The Connection Method®

CREATE AN IMPACTFUL *brand* THROUGH THE POWER OF *connection*

KELSEY KURTIS

Dedicated to The Connection Crew.

For being fearless in your pursuit to connect with yourself and use your Connection-Based Brand so others can feel seen, feel heard and remind them that they matter.

TABLE OF CONTENTS

PART 3 *Using Your Brand*

PREFACE

This is where it started...

PREFACE

This book was an accident.

An honest-to-goodness accident.

I always thought that writing a book was a romantic notion, but wondered, "What the hell would I write about?!" However, that all changed in January 2019. A woman approached me after I spoke at an event and asked me to help her define her brand for her new business.

I agreed and got to work on what I expected to be a be a simple 10-page workbook to guide her through the branding process. Instead, I ended up creating a new perspective on branding, and a completely new concept called Connection-Based Branding.

Instead of 10 pages, I ended up writing 100+ pages of the first draft of the book you now hold in your hands.

I guess it's the truth when they say, "Write what you know," because once I sat down at the computer to write about the way I approach branding, the floodgates opened.

I never intended to write a book, but sometimes your purpose calls you to the side of the pool and pushes you into the deep end, whether you are ready or not. And no, I wasn't ready when this opportunity heaved her heavy, concrete ass onto my lap. No, I wasn't ready at all. None of us ever are.

However, I've found that ignoring direct prompts from your purpose never ends well.

My biggest mentor, Oprah Winfrey, says, "You have one job in life, and that is to find your purpose and get to the business of doing it."

I had been searching for my purpose, and here she was, busting down my door. I listened, and here we are.

To give you a little background, I began my relationship with branding, business, and entrepreneurship early on in my life.

When I was 11 years old, my Grandpa Paul, pulled me aside and said, "Kelsey, it's time to start your first business!"

I considered my Grandpa Paul a master entrepreneur. During the glory days of Hollywood, he owned a successful florist business in downtown Los Angeles. He also co-owned a sailboat brokerage with his brothers in Newport Beach, CA. He had always been passionate about business and serving others and his community through his business ventures.

As a kid, I played every business imaginable. I had an imaginary video rental business, a clothing store, a McDonalds, a toy store, and a grocery store. You name it. I was the owner and operator of a new business every day. It was no surprise Grandpa Paul wanted to nurture my blossoming entrepreneurial spirit.

We bypassed the lemonade stand and started my first business. It was called Kelsey's Jewelry. We imported unique silver jewelry from Mexico and wholesaled the pieces to local boutiques and shops.

Kelsey's Jewelry would be where I learned "Grandpa's Way" of doing business. Grandpa Paul had a unique approach to business that flipped my perspective completely upside down from what I thought business was all about.

When we would go on our first sales trips, much to my surprise, Grandpa told me to leave the jewelry in the car. I thought that was strange since the whole purpose was to go in and sell our product, but I was 11 years old, what did I know?

I followed his instruction and proceeded to go into the boutique where we would meet and chat with the shop owner. In these conversations, we introduced ourselves, asked about their story, and I would tell a joke or Grandpa would tell one of his famous stories from his many adventures. Then we would leave—with no mention of the jewelry.

Our second and third sales trips followed this same pattern—chatting and shooting the shit with the shop owner—and no mention of jewelry.

Then, around our fourth time to the boutique, we would bring in the jewelry, and an amazing thing happened. We sold out every tray of jewelry. EVERY. TIME.

I learned this was the secret to Grandpa Paul's business success. He impressed on me the value of connection and relationships and their relation to business growth. Businesses can come and go, but relationships last. He taught me that sound business is rooted in relationships and in order to have a lasting business, you must build from a foundation of human-to-human connection. Start there and everything else falls into place.

Grandpa Paul explained it to me this way, he said: "Kelsey, it's not about the thing you're selling. It's not about the jewelry. It's about the story. Your story. Their story. It's about who you are as a person and why you're doing what you're doing. Let them see you before they see the jewelry. If you do that, the relationship is built, and the sale is done before you even walk into the door."

Little did I know that Grandpa Paul's advice and relationship—first business education would lay the foundation for everything I would do in the future, and everything I am about to share with you in this book.

The Connection Method is rooted in these lessons my Grandfather taught me as well as the experiences I've personally trekked through in my own life and as a business owner. This book also shares my experiences working with countless other leaders and entrepreneurs who I've helped define their own Connection-Based Brand with *The Connection Method* process.

You are a brand, even if you
don't own a business

Just like what my Grandfather did for me, I hope to do for you, and that is, to shift your perspective. *The Connection Method* is about taking the idea of traditional branding and flipping it upside down 180 degrees to look at it from a new point of view. *The Connection Method* is about connecting with others on the human level *first* before your product or service in order to make an intentional impact with your business or leadership role.

The Connection Method is for both entrepreneurs and leaders in a career. It's here to remind you that you are a brand, even if you don't own a business. This book will give you simple and actionable steps to help you get clear on who you are and where you're going, because when you know that, you're more equipped to genuinely connect with others, stand confident in yourself and grow with intention in all areas of life, business and leadership.

That's what's waiting for you in *The Connection Method*.

INTRO
This is where we're going...

INTRODUCTION

We all have a Sasquatch Factor.

You know, that "thing" that makes us feel different, like an outsider or even a curiosity—much like the tall, hairy, and elusive mythical creature of the forest, known as Sasquatch (otherwise known as Bigfoot). That "thing" can be completely obvious, something outwardly physical, or something more deeply rooted within our hearts. That "thing" that we try to repress, hide or dismiss in order to fit in, or are culturally taught to be ashamed of. Whatever it is, it's a unique part of us, of our personal story and makes up the foundation of who we are.

I found my Sasquatch Factor early in life when I realized I wasn't like the other kids at school. Not only did I have a creative imagination and a big personality with a lot of unbridled energy, but I was also the biggest kid in class, both height and weight. I never felt like I belonged to a group of friends who got me. Not until I was in my 30's!

These days, I'm still often the tallest and biggest in a group–especially in a room full of women. I stand six feet tall. I am not slim or stereotypically athletic, and I wear a size 12 shoe (talk about Bigfoot!). Nothing about me physically has ever been average or normal.

I have always been different and was teased, bullied, and made to feel like an outcast because of it. My size, my looks, my outdated thrift store clothes, my creative spirit, and my colorful imagination all were prime targets for ridicule and mockery.

Although these experiences were extremely hurtful, they were invaluable in shaping who I am today. They helped me gain insight and perspective on how to navigate feeling unseen, confused, overwhelmed, and isolated. But most of all, they helped me gain a unique perspective for understanding human behavior. They showed me that no matter the circumstance, everything comes back to one integral human need—*connection*.

For me, as a child and as an adult, I yearned to find and experience true, genuine connection. Connection was my missing piece, the thing that I was searching for. I've found what we lack in our past is what we search for in the now, so as a result, I have spent my life researching and learning how to connect with people.

The truth about the Sasquatch Factor, is that the things that make us different (our personal Sasquatch Factors) turn out to be the main source of connecting with others. When we learn that others have experienced the same struggles, we don't feel like an outcast, instead we feel seen. More on this in a later chapter.

The biggest nugget of truth I have learned in my quest for connection is that the truest form of connection stems from being able to see ourselves in others. Others can be a person, a place, a brand, or a thing.

Think about it for a second.

Imagine the people you have the deepest connections with. Think about the companies or products you are loyal to, and the places that mean the most to you. They ALL have a piece of you. A reflection of you in them in some way. They all touch on something you care about. They all, in whatever way, have reached out and said," You are welcome here, we see you, we hear you, you matter, and you are one of us."

Seeing yourself in others is about connecting with the biggest pieces of someone's or something's story or it can be the smallest, seemingly insignificant pieces. The size of the connection does not determine its value. No matter its size, connection is powerful and provides a path to impact—one that uses your voice, your brand, to help others feel seen, feel heard and know that they matter.

The type of connection we are talking about in *The Connection Method,* is not just any type of connection. The type we will be discussing and building here is genuine. Not one that plays lip service to others to manipulate or that is shrouded in plastic fakery. No, the type of connection we are talking about is the *real* kind that is deep, and heart-centered. The kind of connection that allows you to use your story, your values, and yes, even your Sasquatch Factor to define a brand that is uniquely you and one that deeply resonates with your community.

However, it's impossible to create a genuine connection if you haven't connected with yourself first. If you don't know who you are, what you want, who you want to attract, who you want to surround yourself with, or know the intention behind why you do the things you do, then your connections will lack intention and authenticity.

Without connecting with yourself first you'll end up constantly second guessing your decisions, feeling overwhelmed and allowing the "I'm not good enough" monsters to spin wildly through your head like Tasmanian devils.

Anyone else been there and done that? I know I have!

The Connection Method process is here to help you to take who you are and define it into something tangible and something you can use to combat the self-doubt, the feeling of being scattered without direction, and feeling overwhelmed by the comparison monsters.

You will use *The Connection Method* to define your unique Connection-Based Brand that focuses on connection and serving others.

The 5-step process will guide you through defining your own Connection-Based Brand and to transform your feelings of insecurity into confidence. It will help you communicate exactly who you are, what you value and what others can expect from you. Your Connection-Based Brand will define the narrative so others will know how to perceive you and speak about you.

Once you have defined your Connection-Based Brand you will be able to create the type of impact that stems from your heart, your passion, purpose, and will allow you to genuinely connect.

In *The Connection Method*, you will answer a slew of intentional and deep questions that will create the foundation of your Connection-Based

Brand by defining who you are, what you value, what others can expect, and who you want to attract and serve in your community.

However, to accomplish this, you must be willing to step out from behind the "everything is perfect and impersonal wall" so others can see you. You must be ready to define your values, own your Sasquatch Factor and step out of your comfort zone by sharing your Connection-Based Brand message.

But who is *The Connection Method* for? Who can benefit from defining a Connection-Based Brand?

The Connection Method is for entrepreneurs, business owners and leaders who have big dreams. Leaders who want to create, develop, and leave a lasting impact.

Whether you're just starting a new business, starting a new career, stepping into a leadership role, or you've have been in business or a career for years, defining a Connection-Based Brand will help you move forward towards your goals with intentional direction, clarity and confidence.

Connection-Based Branding is about *bringing humanity back to business*. It's about squashing the old "it's not personal, it's business" mindset and allowing the personal to form the foundation of your brand message.

Connection-Based Branding is founded on one simple concept, that *the truest form of connection comes when others can see themselves in you*. In order to genuinely connect, you first have to get in touch with you. You have to get personal.

Consistency. Confidence. Impact. If you're willing to get personal and do the work, that is what's waiting for you at the end of this book. After going through *The Connection Method* process, you will have created your own Connection-Based Brand that will help keep you consistent and be the foundation to develop confidence.

Consistency breeds confidence. With the consistency your Connection-Based Brand will bring, confidence will not only develop for you, but also your greater community. You will be more confident in making decisions, and your community will be more confident in what you offer as an entrepreneur or leader.

If you are seeking consistency and confidence, are tired of feeling scattered and unsure, and are looking for clarity and direction, you're in the right place. You're here for a reason. Your voice has value, and others need to hear it. *The Connection Method* is here to help you find your voice and define it so you can connect and impact others.

Now's the time to dig deep. Now's the time to connect. Let's go!

PART 1

Branding Basics

CHAPTER ONE

WHAT IS BRANDING?

"Your brand is what other people say about you when you're not in the room."

– JEFF BEZOS, AMAZON FOUNDER & CEO

When I ask someone, "Tell me about your brand," without fail, I get one of two answers back in return.

The first response. They eagerly reach for their wallet and pull out their business card. They excitedly point out the specific design, colors and fonts they chose.

When I ask, "Why did you choose those colors and fonts?", most of the time they come back with "I thought it looked nice," or "It's what everyone else in my industry does." To be clear, yes, branding visuals like your colors, fonts and logo are a part of branding but it isn't the core of what makes a brand.

The second response. They explain, "My brand? Well, yes, I know I need to work on it and improve my social media presence and put myself out there more." This response is not branding at all. It's actually marketing. We'll get into the differences between branding and marketing later on.

However, one thing that both answers prove to me, time and time again, is that most of us don't actually know what branding is.

Everyone throws the word branding around like free candy at a parade, but we don't truly understand it's purpose, meaning or how it applies to our life. All we know is that we need a brand and must partake in this illusive branding thing, so we play along without a true understanding of what it is, how it's formed or what it's used for.

That's why we need to start with the basics and learn about generic branding before we can dig into the ins and outs of what you came here for: the branding perspective and process I've created, Connection-Based Branding.

It's crucial that you have a clear understanding of what branding is, what it isn't and why it's important. In this chapter, we're going to dive into the basics of generic branding. That way you can have a good understanding of how Connection-Based Branding fits into the branding world and how it's different.

BRANDING IS MORE THAN A LOGO: THE 3 ELEMENTS

A brand is composed of three essential elements. These elements can stand on their own, but once defined and put together in a sequential process, they become a powerful tool to help you build consistency, confidence, and intentionality. When combined, these three elements will also be key to build trust, loyalty, and connection with your overall community.

The three elements of a defined brand are:

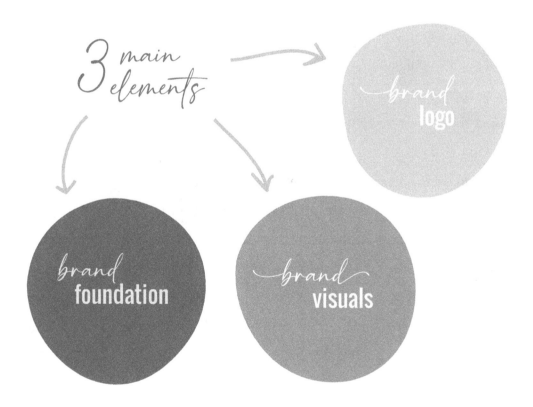

STEP 1: BRAND FOUNDATION

A Brand Foundation is the perceived emotional image of a business or individual. It encompasses who they are, what they value, what others can expect, and their overall mission.

Your Brand Foundation is the heart of your brand. This is what directs every other element of your brand, the direction you go and the decisions you make. This is the compass and map. Your Brand Foundation is literally a box of wet concrete that you place your feet in and say "This is me! This is what I do! This is who I am! This is how I serve! Take it or leave it!" That box of wet concrete, your Brand Foundation, provides the consistency and confidence that is steadfast and solid.

One of the biggest factors of branding is that you define the narrative of how people see you and speak about you. *You* do. However, if you don't define that, you give that power and responsibility to others to define it for you.

If you feel scattered, overwhelmed, or are searching for clarity and direction, chances are you've skipped the all-important first step of defining your Brand Foundation. Don't worry. You aren't the only one. Defining your Brand Foundation requires time, introspection, and decisiveness. It's not the "fun or pretty" part of branding like designing a logo or choosing your colors and fonts. It is actually the step that challenges you and pushes you out of your comfort zone, so most people skip over it.

Defining your Brand Foundation is the most overlooked, yet important step to define in the branding process. If you skip over this step, it results in wasting precious time, energy and resources because you're acting out of impulsivity, not intentionality, and because of this, are more likely to make costly decisions.

Your Brand Foundation is the heart and soul of your brand that leads the next steps for everything else, including the other two elements.

> " Your Brand Foundation is the heart and soul of your brand that leads everything else, including the other two elements. "

This first step, defining your Brand Foundation, is what we will be focused on creating in this book. A Brand Foundation that you can then take with intention into the next two steps, your Branding Visuals and Branding Logo. Instead of making decisions because they "look good" or "look pretty" you can use your Brand Foundation to lead with intention and know why you chose those colors, why you chose that logo, why your website looks the way it does, why you market a specific way and why you connect and attract some people as well as repel others.

The Brand Foundation element is the most important part of a brand, and after a brief introduction to the two other essential brand elements, we are going to focus our full attention on defining and building your own Brand Foundation in the form of your Connection-Based Brand.

STEP 2: BRAND VISUALS

The visual elements to represent your brand.

Brand visuals can be everything from the branding colors you choose, the fonts, website design, photography, to even the interior design of your space. This is the visual identity and visual representation of your brand.

Anything visual that represents your brand first must run through the first element, your Brand Foundation. That way you're making decisions with intention (i.e., knowing why something looks the way it does), because there must be a why behind every choice you make.

In order to create consistency with your Brand Visuals, you must run every decision through your Brand Foundation first.

STEP 3: BRAND LOGO

A simple design marker representing your brand in icon form.

Your brand logo is closely tied into your Brand Visuals but is a separate icon marker to simply represent your brand. A brand logo can be an illustrated design, a text logo, or a hybrid of both. Again, your logo should be something that is defined after you first define your Brand Foundation and then your Brand Visuals. Make sure your logo is aligned with your overall feel and intention behind who you are and how you want others to feel about you and your brand.

BRANDING IS NOT MARKETING

Branding is your message.
Marketing is how that message is delivered.

Earlier I shared the two most common responses to the question, "Tell me about your brand." We now know that branding is more than your business card and a visual design. So, let's talk about the second misconception about branding, that branding is the same as marketing.

Branding and marketing work together but are two separate elements that do two very different things. Simply, branding is your message, and marketing is how that message is delivered.

In order to have a confident and effective marketing plan, you must first start by defining your Brand Foundation. Otherwise, you will continually feel scattered, and like you are just throwing spaghetti at the wall to see what sticks versus being intentional and effective. Marketing is a popular topic, so don't worry, we will dive into discussing marketing later in the book.

WHAT IS BRANDING?
Wrap Up

Now you understand what branding IS and most importantly, is NOT. This is important so when it's time to dive into defining your brand, you will know exactly what you are working towards.

Keep in mind that, unless otherwise stated, moving forward from here and throughout the book, when I refer to a brand, I will be specifically referring to your Brand Foundation.

> " The Connection Method process
> helps you to start fresh and
> define your Brand Foundation. "

That way, once you finish this book, you will have an intentional Brand Foundation that you can use to create branding visuals, your logo, effective marketing strategies and confidently know why you chose these things versus always second guessing yourself.

WHAT IS BRANDING?

In this chapter you learned:

➯ **Branding is more than a logo.**

➯ **Branding is composed of three elements:**

- Your Brand Foundation
- Your Brand Visuals
- Your Brand Logo

➯ **Your Brand Foundation is the heart of your brand. It's the overall perception and message you wish to share with others.**

➯ **Branding is not marketing. Branding is your message and marketing is how that message is delivered.**

➯ **You must define your brand message first in order to have something tangible, consistent and intentional that others can understand and connect with.**

CHAPTER TWO

WHAT IS A CONNECTION-BASED BRAND?

"Don't worry about being successful, but work toward being significant and the success will follow."

- OPRAH WINFREY

I have always challenged the status-quo.

If someone tells me, "well that's just the way it is" my brain starts thinking of a different way of doing it. When I was 4 years old, I only made it through one dance class because I didn't like being told that you had to dance a "certain way."

Yes, I was that kid who was off in the corner twerking like a baby unicorn while the other kids perfectly performed pliés to an eight count. When I studied music, I was unable to read sheet music, so I created my own note patterns which my brain could easily recognize when singing or playing piano.

When given the option of "normal" or doing it "another way," I always choose "another way."

My think-outside-of-the-box thinking has brought us here, to think about branding in a new light. Connection-Based Branding flips traditional branding upside down and views it from a new lens. A lens that focuses on bringing humanity back to business and building a brand that grows and impacts through genuine human connection.

> Connection-Based Branding flips traditional branding upside down and views it from a new lens.

With traditional business branding, the status quo has been that, from the outside, your brand, what you offer and how you offer it must be perfect. Your brand must have an intricately manicured "hedge of perfection" between the business owner or leaders and their audience, customers, and community. Traditional business branding says, "We are a perfect logo and a product, connect with that and that will be enough."

However, with the rise of new technologies and social networks, people are craving for deeper connection, so that perfect "hedge" doesn't cut it anymore.

In today's culture, people are seeking real. They are seeking purpose. They are evaluating the values, the lifestyle and the ethics of the leadership and overall brand mission before making a purchase, collaborating, or before hiring someone new.

Our current culture craves connection. They want to know the human(s) behind a business or organization, they want to know the story. Consumers want to connect more deeply than surface level. They want to buy into something bigger—a cause, a value set, a purpose.

Brands and the people behind them can't hide behind their business card and logo anymore. Their customers and community are calling for more. They are calling for transparency. They are calling for something or someone that they can genuinely connect with; a brand message they can attach to and buy into it.

Traditional branding says to keep business and personal separate. However, look at the most successful leaders and businesses, and you will see that they have learned how to successfully overlap the two. Look at Oprah Winfrey, Richard Branson, Sara Blakely, Taylor Swift, Dwayne Johnson, Will Smith, Chrissy Teigen, Serina Williams and Tyra Banks. They all have built incredibly successful professional brands, businesses, with great impact, while simultaneously integrating humanity and connection by weaving in their personal brand, showing bits and pieces of who they are on a more personal level.

Humans don't connect with perfect; they connect with real. Humans don't connect with superficial; they connect with deep-rooted purpose. Humans don't buy from logos; humans buy from humans.

That's what Connection-Based Branding is all about.

Connection-Based Branding is about bridging the gap between professional and personal, and focused on bringing the human element back to business and leadership. It's about opening a gate just wide enough to allow your community to peek into the mission, values, story and real people behind a brand.

Connection-Based Branding is rooted in the fundamental concept of connection, that the truest form of connection comes from when others can see themselves in you.

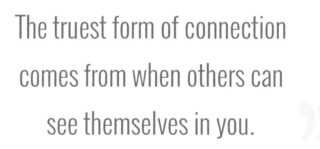

> " The truest form of connection comes from when others can see themselves in you. "

However, if you don't know who you are, it's going to be incredibly hard and extremely difficult to genuinely connect with others and create a memorable brand that creates a lasting impact. But it can be done.

Sara Blakely, the creator, and CEO of SPANX shapewear epitomizes the essence of a Connection-Based Brand.

The SPANX brand was founded on Sara's personal story of creativity, problem solving, hard work, perseverance, and grit. The SPANX product line echoes Sara's values by empowering her customers to feel confident in who they are and to go after their goals while using her product.

On social media, Sara opens her personal life just enough for us to see who she is and allows us to connect with her. We see her making pancakes with her kids on Sundays, and then running her multimillion-dollar company on Monday.

Blakely allows you just enough of a glimpse into her world so she can provide simple moments of human connection. When her kids walk out the door with two different shoes, you say, "Yep, I've had that kind of day too!" or "Yep, those are my kids too!" When you share simple moments of connection, that's when genuine connection, trust and loyalty starts to blossom.

That mismatched shoes moment may seem small and insignificant, but after spending time connecting with Blakely on social media, when it comes time to buy shapewear, you're going to remember the times she opened up her heart to you. You're going to remember the mismatched shoe moment, and how you felt seen and connected. And in the end, chances are, you're going to grab the SPANX brand over another shapewear.

That is how Connection-Based Branding works.

Whether you own a business or are a leader within an organization, your personal values and your personal story will directly integrate into your business or career allowing you to deeply connect with your community, coworkers, and/or customers. Your personal values and story will be the driving force behind what you do, both personally and professionally, and how you present your brand to the world. It will be the tangible piece connecting you to your community.

The core purpose of Connection-Based Branding is to bridge the gap between personal and professional and has four main goals:

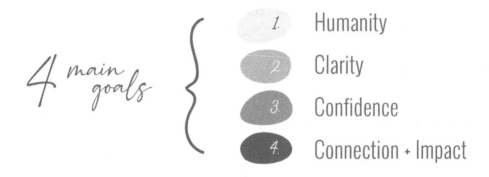

4 main goals { 1. Humanity 2. Clarity 3. Confidence 4. Connection + Impact

1. HUMANITY

Connection-Based Branding is about humans connecting with humans. Business and leadership aren't only about the product you sell or the job you do. They're about the people behind them. People buy you first before your product. People buy your story before hiring you. It always comes back to the human element.

Humans buy from humans. Humans hire humans. Humans are the driving force behind a brand, and the human element is where connection is built. Connection-Based Branding allows space for the human element to exist and thrive within what you offer.

2. CLARITY

Defining your Connection-Based Brand will help give you clarity in a world full of options, opinions, and ideas. It will help you step out of feeling scattered and step into feeling confident, allowing you to lead with intentionality instead of impulsivity.

With a clear plan, you can share your brand message with intentionality. You can create brand visuals that have meaning and intentionality. Your Connection-Based Brand will be a road map of clarity to your next step and a path for creating consistency in your decisions and next moves.

I once worked with a large corporate client, and in our initial meeting together, I asked them about their current brand. They said that they had a 30-page document outlining their brand message. I looked at them wide eyed and realized why they had called me in. A 30-page document is not the ideal tool to help them and their team with a clear and simple game plan while in the trenches of building the business and their team's individual careers.

When the leadership, employees, or contractors are experiencing self-doubt or feeling overwhelmed with not knowing what decision to make, a 30-page document will not be the place they go to for clarity and direction. No, branding must be simple, clear, and actionable.

That's what *The Connection Method* and defining a Connection-Based Brand can create for you. Something that is clear, direct, and summarized. Something that you can quickly refer to, to give you and your team which offers instant and effective clarity for the next steps.

3. CONFIDENCE

As you gain clarity by defining your Connection-Based Brand, and start consistently implementing your brand, confidence can start to blossom.

Defining your Connection-Based Brand is your permission slip to be yourself. Your Connection-Based Brand will be a source of validation for who you are and what you are doing. Your Connection-Based Brand will take the road map of clarity and empower you—the person(s) behind the brand—with a plan for consistency. When you are consistent, your confidence is able to grow and thrive. This confidence allows you to not only stand securely in who you are, but also helps build the confidence others have in you in your overall community.

4. CONNECT + IMPACT

Our current culture is craving connection. People are hidden behind screens, operating in a virtual world, feeling lonely and wondering if they belong. Defining and sharing your Connection-Based Brand provides a powerful opportunity to reach these people on a human level. It allows you to genuinely connect.

When you do this, it opens the door to create a bigger impact in your community. It opens up the door for you to help others feel seen, feel heard, and know that they matter by connecting with your story and your brand message. When you connect on this deep level, that's how long-term impact can be made in your community and beyond.

This is the ultimate goal of why we are here.

WHO IS CONNECTION-BASED BRANDING FOR?

It's a common misconception that individuals who don't own their own business don't need to define their brand. The truth is, Connection-Based Branding is not reserved exclusively for entrepreneurs or business owners. It's also for leaders.

Leaders in all forms.

A Connection-Based Brand is for leaders who desire to make an impact in their industry, connect with their communities, inspire others, and inspire change. Whether you are a visionary entrepreneur, own your own business, or are a leader within an organization as an employee, Connection-Based Branding will help empower you to define your voice, and stand confident in who you are.

Let's look into the two main groups who can benefit from *The Connection Method* and defining a Connection-Based Brand:

1. The Entrepreneur/Business Owner
2. The Leader in an Organization/Community.

ENTREPRENEUR/BUSINESS OWNER

An entrepreneur is someone who has the 'big idea" vision and is the one who takes the risk to see that idea come to fruition. A business owner is the one that oversees an already established company or organization. Most business owners start off as an entrepreneur and then, as their idea and vision grow, naturally step into a business owner role. That's why they are generally synonymous.

A Connection-Based Brand will help give entrepreneurs and business owners clear direction in the early stages of vision development or re-envisioning their business. Having the ability to ask the questions now versus later will save not only time, energy, and resources in the long run, but also provides emotional support as they experience the growing pains and mind games a new idea or venture can bring.

By using their Connection-Based Brand, entrepreneurs/business owners will be equipped to make intentional business structure and growth decisions that stay consistent within their overall values, vision, and goals, versus making decisions purely on emotion, impulsivity, and desperation. Doing this work now is incredibly vital for laying the foundation for brand development and progression to building a brand culture and legacy.

Having a Connection-Based Brand will help entrepreneurs/business owners and their team clearly communicate the brand mission and purpose as a business. It allows for consistency, so their audience knows what to expect and what they are buying into. It will help them decide what type of marketing and branding visuals to create for their business and help scale with intention. Don't worry, this will be covered more in depth later on in the book.

LEADER IN ORGANIZATION/COMMUNITY

Being a leader is a mindset, not your job description. Leaders have long-term vision. They want to be a part of supporting and growing a certain culture, project, or movement. Whether this leader holds a job at a small business, a seat at a corporation, a position in a nonprofit, or has a role in local government or in their community, they can see the bigger picture. I refer to this type of person as a "leader in an organization" or "leader in a community" versus "employee."

> ## Being a leader is a mindset, not your job description.

The differentiating factor between a leader and employee is mindset. A person can be both a leader and an employee at the same time, but it's their vision and desire to create an impact that allows them to have long term goals. These may include seeking growth and bigger opportunities outside of their current circumstance. They see beyond just the short-term paycheck and can evaluate the opportunities (or even lack thereof) around them to see where they can progress or even if it is time to move on.

Keep in mind a leader's current job title is of no consequence. A leader in an organization can be a top-level executive at Taco Bell Corporate or can be someone who works the drive-thru window at a Taco Bell restaurant. The title doesn't matter, being a leader is a mindset, not your job description.

You are a brand, even if you don't own a business.

If you're a leader in an organization/community, and you have goals to advance your life and career, you need to define your own Connection-

Based Brand. When you do, you can use your personal Connection-Based Brand narrative to help you create a kick-ass resume, to show up ready and confident at an interview, and you're able to step up and ask for that promotion or lead a team. It all comes back to knowing your own brand and defining exactly who you are and what you bring to the table. When you have that, you're able to be more empowered to confidently progress forward in both life and leadership!

CONNECTION-BASED BRANDING IS <u>NOT</u> FOR YOU

I hope you were encouraged and felt seen by one of the two main groups *The Connection Method* can help. We will go into even more detail about who Connection-Based Branding is for next, but I want to take a quick moment to address specifically who this book and process is NOT for.

I am very particular about who enters this Connection-Based Brand Community, so if you're transaction focused and not relationship focused, this might not be the resource for you. If you do not desire to invest time in building relationships but are just looking to make a quick buck or find a new "scheme," Connection-Based Branding is definitely *not for you*!

If you identify with any of the following characteristics, please put this book back or send it back to where it came from and walk away.

This book is not for you if you are...

⇨ An individual who is looking to use a false sense of connection in order to take advantage of others to advance their personal gains without regard to others.

⇨ An individual focused on self—not service.

⇨ An individual who is focused on short term gain, not long-term impact.

⇨ An individual content with complacency and mediocrity.

⇨ An individual who is not willing to step out of their comfort zone.

⇨ An individual who operates through manipulation not inspiration.

⇨ An individual who is not willing to connect with themselves in order to connect with others.

If your values and intentions for your actions don't align with the values of Connection-Based Branding, then *The Connection Method* is not for you. Thanks for hanging out with me this long, but I think it's time we say goodbye for now. Good luck!

CONNECTION-BASED BRANDING IS FOR YOU

If you didn't connect with any of the items on previous list, then you are definitely in the right place! If you need a little extra validation to make sure this book is for you, go through the following characteristics checklist to confirm that *The Connection Method* process and Connection-Based Branding can be beneficial for you:

⇨ An individual who doesn't necessarily feel like a leader but has a desire to impact and inspire others.

⇨ An individual who is overwhelmed by all the options and needs a way to make intentional decisions.

⇨ An individual who feels scattered with all the "things "and wants direction.

⇨ An individual who desires consistency.

⇨ An individual who desires confidence.

⇨ An individual who wants to share their story in order to help others.

⇨ An individual who wants to lead with service.

⇨ An individual willing to step out of their comfort zone and do the work.

⇨ An individual who genuinely wants to connect with their community.

⇨ An individual who wants to leave a lasting legacy.

THE CONNECTION CREW

If you said "Yes! That's me!" to any of the preceding characteristics checklist, then you are in the right place! Wahoo!!

Come on over! We have a seat at the table with your name on it because you're now officially a part of *The Connection Crew*!

The Connection Crew is a community of individuals who share the same values and vision for positively impacting their industry and community by leading with intention and connection!

We are so glad you are here! Welcome to the Crew!

WHAT IS CONNECTION-BASED BRANDING?
Wrap Up

Whether you're an entrepreneur/business owner or a leader in an organization, the fact you're here means you desire to create something different from traditional branding. You desire to connect with others, and are ready to define a Connection-Based Brand!

> " You're here because you're ready to embark on a journey to connect with yourself so you can best connect with others—because that's where true connection happens. "

You're here because you desire to step out of feeling scattered and wish to have a clear path for consistency and confidence. You're committed to taking time to build long term relationships through connection versus finding the quick and short-term path.

You're here because you're ready to do the work to step out of your comfort zone and step into creating intentional impact in your community by sharing your brand message.

You're here because you're ready to embark on a journey to connect with yourself so you can best connect with others—because that's where true connection happens. I am grateful you're here and am excited to go on this journey with you!

WHAT IS A CONNECTION-BASED BRAND?

In this chapter you learned:

⇨ What is a Connection-Based Brand and how it's different from traditional branding.

⇨ You learned that Connection-Based branding is about bridging the gap between the professional and the personal, and that defining your Connection-Based Brand is your permission slip to be yourself.

⇨ You learned that the four main goals of defining a Connection-Based Brand is

- Humanity
- Clarity
- Confidence
- Connect + Impact

⇨ You learned who Connection-Based Branding is not for.

⇨ You learned who Connection-Based Branding is for.

⇨ You learned that Connection-Based Branding is for individuals who desire to connect with others and impact their community. It's for entrepreneurs/business owners, leaders in an organization/community.

⇨ You learned about our community, The Connection Crew!

CHAPTER THREE

BENEFITS OF A CONNECTION-BASED BRAND

"If you don't give the market the story to talk about, they'll define your brand's story for you."

- DAVID BRIER, AUTHOR

Social scientist, Dr. Brené Brown, shared that "when we name and own hard things, it does not give them power, it gives us power." As Dr. Brown suggests, we must take the intangible "hard things" and make them tangible by naming or defining them.

In business and leadership, I consider the "hard things" to be our brain ramblings, overwhelming feelings, the uncertainty, the anxiety, and the decisions we must make in our life, business and/or our leadership role.

When you name the hard things, the struggles, overthinking, fears and emotions, and give them a real, tactile existence, this is when you can claim or reclaim power for yourself.

The defining process is exactly what *The Connection Method* branding process provides. When you define a Connection-Based Brand with *The Connection Method*, you gain power and permission to be you. Defining your Connection-Based Brand provides so much more than traditional branding and surface level "brand recognition," it provides both emotional and tangible support to help you navigate your role as a leader within your business, community and/or organization.

There are six key benefits of defining your Connection-Based Brand. You will:

⇨ Gain a map of clarity

⇨ Gain consistency & confidence

⇨ Defines the narrative

⇨ Lay the foundation for legacy

⇨ Know where to spend your resources

⇨ Become a Connection-Based Leader

BENEFIT 1:
GAIN A MAP OF CLARITY

Alex Honnold is one of the best rock climbers in the world. In 2017, he successfully completed the first-ever, free-solo climb of the 2,000-foot

(610 meters) Freerider wall of El Capitan in Yosemite National Park.

Free-solo climbing is unique in that it meant Honnold would climb this sheer rock wall, which was taller than *two* Eiffel Towers stacked on top of one another, without any ropes. You read that correctly, absolutely no safety ropes at all. If he missed a foothold or misplaced a finger and fell … that's it. He's dead.

This was a seemingly impossible human feat, but he accomplished this years-in-the-making the climb in just under 4 hours on June 3, 2017, completely unscathed. Honnold attributed his success to his preparation. He said, "If I'm gonna do it, I need a map."

His preparation led him to create a custom map of the route he would take up the wall and then choreographed each of his movements with precision. Like a dance, every movement was intentional and memorized. He studied, he practiced, and he remained consistent. He stayed committed to his map and plan.

His consistency paid off, by not only providing him a tangible plan for going up the wall, but also the emotional confidence he needed to make a successful climb. Both a logical map and emotional confidence were vital elements to his success.

Could you imagine if Alex just decided one day, "I'm going to free-solo climb El Capitan with no ropes or preparation and see we'll see how it goes?!" Without preparation and intention, we all know it would have ended his life. Creating a clear map for where he was going, and being committed to that map, was the reason he was successful and is alive today.

This is how you need to approach defining your Connection-Based Brand.

Your personal mental and physical wellness along with professional success depend on having a clear direction for knowing where you're currently at and creating a plan for where you are going.

We are all guilty of jumping headfirst into a project, a business, a job, or leading a team without a plan. We arrive at our own El Capitan without a map, and dive in without intention, direction, or clear goals. This often leaves us feeling scattered, frustrated, stressed, uncertain, and like we've misused our time and money. One of the most gratifying benefits of defining your Connection-Based Brand is that it provides simplistic clarity, like a map telling you where to go so you can leave feeling scattered and unsure behind.

> " One of the most gratifying benefits of defining your Connection-Based Brand is that it provides simplistic clarity, like a map telling you where to go. "

After working with so many entrepreneurs and leaders on defining their Connection-Based Brand, the one thing they all say after we work together is, "I now have a clear direction to where I'm going. I have such clarity and confidence! I don't feel scattered because I know where I'm at and where I'm heading!"

Defining your Connection-Based Brand will be your map of clarity for how to navigate which direction you go. It will help you navigate the emotions, overthinking, and decisions you encounter on the daily. It will act as a discerning filter for each crossroad you encounter and each decision you need to make.

BENEFIT 2:
GAIN CONSISTENCY + CONFIDENCE

I once met a woman who remodeled and designed her home around a single silver bracelet. This bracelet was a stunning heirloom piece at least 80 years old. The base was silver and was accented with cream, brown, turquoise, and shiny mercury glass beads. She said this bracelet captured the essence of her; a little down to earth, a little bit funky and a splash of sparkle.

When she had the opportunity to remodel her home, the only inspiration and guidance she gave the designers was this bracelet. She told them, "This is what the house should look like. From the new walls, cabinets, colors, finishes and decor, I want this home to be a reflection of this bracelet. If you can do that, this home will be a visual extension of me."

The designer took the bracelet and filtered every design decision through it. The light fixtures were mercury glass. The paint and finishing's had a warm neutral tone. The pillows were turquoise for a pop of color. Everything was tied back to the bracelet.

Using this bracelet, she branded her home.

When you walk into this woman's home, you know who she is. You feel her heart and style. You feel the essence of her in her home. She stayed consistent to something that represented her, therefore creating a space that communicated who she was without having to say a word.

Just like creating a space around a bracelet, this is how you will build consistency and confidence for yourself and what you offer. By using your Connection-Based Brand message as your "bracelet" you will define your brand message and filter everything through it, and I mean ... everything! That is the only way to stay consistent and avoid getting distracted.

You will filter everything through your Connection-Based Brand such as how you visually present your brand with your logo, colors, fonts, overall aesthetic, and even how you market your brand. In addition, you will also filter the way you speak about yourself and how you speak to others, the way you lead, the decisions you make, the opportunities you take, even down to the way you dress will be filtered and defined by the elements of your Connection-Based Brand.

When you filter everything through your Connection-Based Brand, consistency has a place to thrive.

Consistency will be your secret weapon for success. Inconsistency is costing you. It is costing you clients. It is costing you jobs and promotions. It is costing you opportunities. It is costing you personally in wellness and growth. It is costing you—period.

To avoid inconsistency, staying consistent in your Connection-Based Brand message will be the key to help you stand confident in who you are and what you offer. Consistency will also take away the guesswork and provide a path for confidence to grow.

" Consistency breeds confidence. "

Consistency is where confidence can start to develop. Consistency breeds confidence. Consistency is the root system where confidence can sprout, blossom, and thrive. Consistency is the key that unlocks the confidence lock.

If you want to be confident, you need to create a pathway of consistency, and that pathway is created by defining your Connection-Based Brand. Whatever role you hold in life, you want to be confident in it.

You don't want to live in the constant cycle of second guessing yourself. You want to feel validated that you're "doing it right" so you can confidently move onto the next step, and then the next, and the next. Your Connection-Based Brand will be a key source of validation for you.

It seems that no matter who I talk to, everyone is looking for more confidence in some way. However, one of the blocks we throw onto our own path is the fear that if we are confident, we will be perceived as cocky, or that we will exude an "I'm better than you" arrogance.

So, let's put this fear to rest. Let's pick up shovels together, dig the grave, and put a red rose on the pile of dirt that contains the fear of appearing cocky if you allow confidence to grow and thrive.

The best way to squash the fear of appearing cocky is to know the difference between the two. The difference between cocky and confidence is quite simple. Cocky is rooted in insecurity, while confidence is rooted in authenticity.

Cocky is rooted out of insecurity, inauthenticity, and fear. Cocky is about masking real and replacing it with fake. Cocky is focused on self-serving vs serving others.

Confidence, on the other hand, is rooted in authenticity. It's rooted in real. An authenticity which can be achieved by having a clear vision of who you are, what you offer, where you're going so you can best serve others.

cocky vs. confident

COCKY   CONFIDENCE

⇧   ⇧

INSECURITY   AUTHENTICITY

Real confidence thrives when you know who you are and serve others with your gifts, passion, and message. Real confidence is sparked and maintained by having consistency and a plan. Consistency comes from creating a plan based on who you authentically are. That plan is your Connection-Based Brand.

Working with my clients and community and seeing their transformation from scattered to focused and insecure to confident by just defining their Connection-Based Brand is truly the best part of this process. The feedback I have received from my clients after going through *The Connection Method* has been so inspiring!

"It helped me realize that being me was enough."

"Not only have I become confident in what I do, I am more confident in the firm I represent."

"I feel more confident and rooted in what is important to me and what I can give myself permission to let go or walk away from. Realizing I get to curate the type of clients I want to work with was huge! I also feel more confident that my identity is what I decide—not someone else."

"I feel way more confident about my brand now! My brand is not someone else's ideas being forced on me, it truly is a reflection of me. It's given me the tools to recognize the core of me! Now it feels easy to run with what I've created and feel really confident about what I'm doing now!"

"I had no idea who I was or what I wanted. Then I defined my Connection-Based Brand. I was able to get unstuck and

step into what I really wanted to do. It took time, but it all started with The Connection Method."

Going through *The Connection Method* and defining your Connection-Based Brand, will give you the tools to stay consistent so you can step out of insecurity and stand confident in who you are and what you offer. And when you stay true to you, you don't ever have to worry about coming off as "cocky." You and your brand will be authentically you and be ready to confidently connect with your community.

BENEFIT 3:
DEFINES THE NARRATIVE

I got divorced at 32 years old.

I never thought I would be a statistic. I never thought I would be "that woman" who couldn't see blatant lies right in front of her face. But I was.

After seven years of marriage my husband and I decided to separate. I moved out of our home to give us each the space we needed. We were actively working on our relationship and in counseling trying to figure out our next steps.

However, shortly after I moved out, I spontaneously ran into my husband and his (not known to me) longtime girlfriend and her kids at the movie theater.

I was in shock.

I had no idea.

The next day, I went over to our home and found out that that in just the few weeks since we separated and I moved out, his girlfriend and her kids had moved into our home, was driving our car and was fully aware that he was still married.

Insert brain explosion emoji here because that's exactly how I felt.

I was completely blindsided.

Learning the truth of the situation was traumatizing. However, it also was the most empowering experience because it gave me complete clarity and confidence knowing that our marriage was done. Like nail in the coffin, cemented feet, thrown into the river d-o-n-e.

After I took time to emotionally process this situation, and evaluate my next steps in life, I knew it was time to go public with the divorce. No one, except my immediate family and closest friends knew what was going on.

Before I did though, I took time to lay out what I wanted to say and how I wanted to say it. I needed to take the emotional and turn it into something tangible. I wanted to be empowered with my story not immobilized.

I wanted to be intentional, classy, and empowered. I needed to "brand" my story. So, I went through some of the questions of the very first draft of *The Connection Method* to define what was happening, who I was in that moment, what I valued, where I was going and what people could expect from me moving forward.

Because of *The Connection Method* process, I had the power to define the narrative of my story and how others saw me and spoke about me. It wasn't going to be the other way around.

Through this, I knew that there was no need to be fearful of what others thought of me and my story. I knew that if I lead with intention and not impulsivity with my message, I could simultaneously share my story and impact others with my story at the same time. I could share the truth via the narrative I chose, not one that others pushed upon me.

During my reflection, I decided that this narrative was to be one of hope not helplessness. A narrative that I was a victor not a victim. I wanted to be seen as classy, and not a scorned, bitter woman. And most importantly, I wanted to share the possibilities that emerge from pain and choosing to move forward with positivity and perseverance. That's the narrative I delivered, and that's the narrative that was received. Defining the narrative is one of the most powerful benefits of defining your Connection-Based Brand. The Fear of Others' Opinions can be silenced, since YOU tell people how they should see you and speak about you, not them.

> " You tell people how they should see you and speak about you, not them. "

One of the most used statements (and absolute truths) about branding is that "if you're not branding yourself, you can be sure others do it for you."

Whether you own a business or are a leader in an organization, with your Connection-Based Brand, you have the tool to define the message.

The Connection Method offers you a process to help you define your unique narrative, so you can tell others how to perceive you and speak about you, not the other way around. You define the narrative—not them.

BENEFIT 4:
KNOW WHERE TO SPEND YOUR RESOURCES

You have unlimited amounts of time, energy and financial resources at your disposal, right? Ha! I could barely make it through writing that sentence before busting out laughing at the lunacy of it!

We all know that the opposite is the actual truth.

The real deal is that we have limited time, energy, and resources to achieve a goal. And yet, we're all guilty of jumping into a project without a map and end up wasting a lot of valuable time and money. We end up overworked from accepting projects that aren't a good fit, spending time and money attracting the wrong people, and wasting energy on things that aren't helping us reach our end goal.

So how do we figure out where to allot our most precious commodities of time, energy, and financial resources in order to get the best return?

Like a Spandexed superhero, that's where Connection-Based Branding comes flying in to save the day by providing you both clear direction and validation for where you need to devote your most precious resources.

Using my own Connection-Based Brand, I have decided what podcasts, programs, or stages to speak on, what clients to take on or pass on (or even the ones to let go of), what products or services to invest in, and even the type of team members I bring in to support me and my business.

Anything that requires any ounce of my time, energy or resources, runs through my Connection-Based Brand filter first.

By using your Connection-Based Brand as a filter, you stay consistent, stay on budget, stay energized, and most importantly stay on track with your overall goals.

Your Connection-Based Brand is there to direct your decisions, so that you can be intentional and responsible with the resources you have.

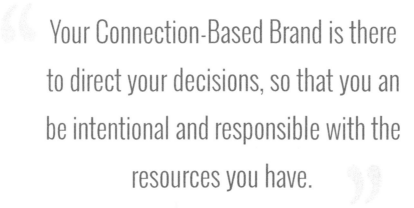

> Your Connection-Based Brand is there to direct your decisions, so that you an be intentional and responsible with the resources you have.

BENEFIT 5:
LAY THE FOUNDATION FOR LEGACY

What's the big picture reason for defining a Connection-Based Brand? What are the growth possibilities from where you start today to where you can grow in the future? The first step of Connection-Based Branding is to connect with yourself so you can connect with others, but where can that connection go? How can it evolve?

The potential growth and impact trajectory can be illustrated by the Connection-Based Brand Evolution.

Each of us have our own vision for how our Connection-Based Brands will grow and develop over time. The Evolution is meant to give you a preview of the kind of impact your Connection-Based Brand is capable of creating. It's meant to give you a big picture glimpse into the possibilities of what you're about to create.

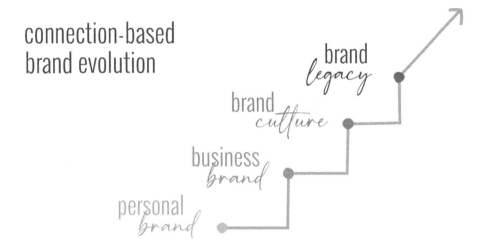

Keep in mind that everyone's level of impact is going to be different. The size of your impact does not determine your value. Some of us dream of creating impact on an interpersonal level or within a small group. Some of us dream of creating impact locally or statewide. Some of us have goals of creating national or global impact with our Connection-Based Brand.

No matter the scale, your goals for impact have value and are completely attainable as long as you start with a solid Connection-Based Brand foundation. That foundation is step one, your PERSONAL BRAND.

PERSONAL BRAND

No matter if you are an individual, team leader or company, Connection-Based Branding first starts at the personal level.

Every great business or leader started here. They started with just an idea, a dream for something bigger and the drive to get it done. Defining your Personal Brand is the first step in the Evolution, the space where you define and create your brand foundation based on your personal values and vision.

Consider Walt Disney. Today, The Walt Disney Company is a multibillion-dollar entertainment corporation, but it didn't start out that way. It first started with one man's dream. It started with Walt Disney's vision for creating innovative and imaginative animations, valuing high quality work, and always focused on moving forward despite failure or roadblocks. It started with his personal brand.

Now you might not have global impact dreams like Disney did, but that doesn't matter. The process is still the same. No matter their size or how they grow, your goals have value, but you must always start at the personal brand level. Once your personal brand is defined, the Connection-Based Branding Evolution can start growing and progressing to something bigger.

As you start owning your Personal Brand, implementing consistency, developing confidence and sharing who you are and what you offer with your Community, your Business Brand can start to take shape.

BUSINESS BRAND

A Business Brand is when others in your immediate circle, industry and community start to take notice and buy into what you're offering. A Business Brand is applicable to both business owners and leaders within an organization/community because a Business Brand can be something you own (like a business) or an offering and service you bring to your industry (like in a career). A Business Brand is when your consistent efforts start to make ripples, so others start to take notice, they start to view you as an expert and start to buy into what you offer.

As those ripples grow bigger and bigger, the third step of the Brand Evolution can start to develop, Brand Culture.

BRAND CULTURE

Brand Culture is when others outside of your immediate industry and community circle start to take notice of what you are offering. They not only buy into what you offer, but deeply connect to a desire to advance the overall mission behind why you're doing it.

Brand Culture starts to evolve when others understand your vision, take ownership of it, and are inspired to advance it on their own.

Brand Culture starts to evolve when others feel a genuine connection to your brand message and your story for why you're doing it. They have reached a point where they trust you, are loyal and are motivated to advance your message.

Individuals in a Brand Culture can be customers, employees, industry peers and beyond. Brand Culture takes hold when others become emotionally connected to your mission and offering. They often times become evangelists for your Connection-Based Brand because they have bought into your message and are personally connected.

As your Brand Culture grows, it takes on a life and following of its own. As it matures and solidifies into your community (and beyond), you and your brand are primed and ready to head towards the last step of the brand evolution, which is your Brand Legacy.

BRAND LEGACY

Brand Legacy is when your brand has progressed through the Connection-Based Brand Evolution Process and has grown and created a larger impact beyond you. It has blossomed into a brand that lives beyond you, a brand that can carry on your message and continue to make an impact. Don't let the word "legacy" intimidate you. A Brand Legacy can be small, interpersonal, and localized, or it can have a global reach.

It doesn't matter the size of the legacy you leave, it only matters that you stepped out, served others, impacted your community and left something lasting that others can connect to and benefit from. It matters that you were a leader, a Connection-Based Leader, whose message of connection allowed others to feel seen, feel heard and know that they mattered. That is Brand Legacy, and that is the kind of impact that awaits.

BENEFIT 6:
BECOME A CONNECTION-BASED LEADER

As I hinted, becoming a Connection-Based Leader is a powerful way to connect with others, share and grow your brand, as well as create a long-lasting Brand Legacy.

Being a Connection-Based Leader allows you to express your Connection-Based Brand on an interpersonal level by being a vessel of connection, a source to inspire others to grow and achieve more. As a Connection-Based Leader, you have the opportunity to be a beacon of light for someone when they might not receive it from anywhere else.

To connect with others and to feel connected is the deepest need of every human on earth. With the age of social media, digital communications and, as I am writing this, the global COVID-19 pandemic, the need for connection is greater than it has ever been.

The goal of a Connection-Based Leader is to use your voice and Connection-Based Brand message to connect with others and meet their three basic human needs. Those three needs are:

We need to feel *seen*

We need to feel *heard*

We need to feel that we *matter*

If a human can feel these three things from another individual (or even a company, product, or organization), that's the foundation for impact. That's the foundation for connection, trust, and loyalty, and that's the goal of a Connection-Based Leader.

A Connection-Based Leader can only develop, connect, and serve effectively if they have defined who they are, what they value, and what people can expect from them. If they have defined a Connection-Based Brand, they must operate with consistency so others can connect with something steadfast, not scattered or insecure.

As I have said before, the truest form of connection comes from when others see themselves in you. So as a leader, you need to know who you are so you can genuinely connect.

The Connection Method provides you an opportunity to dig deep and learn about who you are. It offers you a chance to answer questions that will help you define the kind of leader you are now and who you want to become.

Just like with the word "legacy," don't be intimidated by the word "leader." Yes, a leader can be someone who stands at a podium and speaks to the masses, but a leader can also lead and impact a small group. A leader's value is not determined by the number of people that they lead, their value comes from how they connect, serve, and treat others. Their value comes from how they make others feel. Their value comes from the ability to genuinely make others feel seen, heard and know that they matter.

That's the power of a Connection-Based Leader. That's the potential that awaits you as you define your Connection-Based Brand with *The Connection Method*.

BENEFITS OF A DEFINED BRAND
Wrap-Up

No matter if you are a business owner or a leader within an organization, defining your Connection-Based Brand will be so beneficial for both your personal and professional goals.

Your Connection-Based Brand gives you a map of clarity to create a plan and ability to navigate the options, decisions and ideas thrown your way.

With this map of clarity, your Connection-Based Brand provides you with a path for consistency when developing and sharing your brand message. That consistency empowers you to feel confident in who you are and what you offer. The consistency will also be a way for your community to feel confident in you and start seeing you as the expert.

Your Connection-Based Brand defines the narrative. It takes back the power from the Fear of Others' Opinions and allows you to tell others how you want them to see you, perceive you and speak about you. You define the narrative of who you are and what you offer—not them.

Your Connection-Based Brand helps you be intentional with where to spend your precious time, energy, and financial resources.

And finally, no matter how big or small, your Connection-Based Brand provides a path to greater impact in your community and industry, it lays the foundation for legacy. A legacy that lives beyond you. By going through the Branding Evolution process and creating a legacy, you will develop your role as a Connection-Based Leader.

A Connection-Based Leader's goal is to connect. It is to see others, hear others and make others know that they matter. Not that their money matters, but them, as a person. The first step of becoming a Connection-Based Leader and reaping the benefits of defining and owning your Connection-Based Brand all starts in the next chapter by diving headfirst into *The Connection Method*!

BENEFITS OF A DEFINED CONNECTION-BASED BRAND

In this chapter you learned about The Six Benefits of a Defined Connection-Based Brand :

⇨   **Map of Clarity**

⇨   **Consistency + Confidence**

⇨   **Defines the Narrative**

⇨   **Know where to spend your resources**

⇨   **Lay the foundation for legacy with the Connection-Based Brand Evolution**

⇨   **Becoming a Connection-Based Leader**

connection-based
brand evolution

brand
legacy

brand
culture

business
brand

personal
brand

PART 2

The Connection Method

CHAPTER FOUR

BEFORE YOU START: THE RULES

"It's not hard because you're doing it wrong. It's hard because you're finally doing it RIGHT."

- GLENNON DOYLE, AUTHOR

It's time to finally dive into The Connection Method process and defining your Connection-Based Brand. Wahoo! Break out the kazoos! We finally made it!

I am so excited for you, because you are about to dive deep into the action steps for defining your own, custom-to-you, Connection-Based Brand. It's time to roll up your sleeves, dig in, and dig deep.

Before you get rolling, I wanted to share a few tips, tricks, and recommendations to help you get the most out of *The Connection Method,* as well as invaluable suggestions for mindset.

First, be aware that you will learn quite a few new terms and concepts during this process. I have created a Glossary of Terms in the back of the book for quick reference if you need a refresh on the meanings of certain words or concepts.

Secondly, let's address the potential mind blocks that may show up as you go through *The Connection Method.*

After working with countless leaders on their brand, the same blocks, negative self-talk, fears, overthinking, and confusion consistently rear their ugly heads. So, here are a few suggestions ... no, we are going to call them *rules* you need to be aware of and commit to in order to set yourself up for success as you go through *The Connection Method.*

Keep these rules at the forefront of your mind as you work through this book and please refer back to them when you feel stuck or overwhelmed.

RULE 1:
GIVE YOURSELF GRACE

Building anything that is long lasting requires time, consistency, and a lot of trial and error. Building your Connection-Based Brand is no different. Give yourself grace and patience as you grow, flex, and shift during this process.

Give yourself grace with your reading and processing expectations. We all work, process, and create differently, so there is no "wrong way" to go through *The Connection Method.*

Some may read through the entire book and then go back to work through the questions. Others may read the book and work through the questions simultaneously, not moving onto a new chapter until the previous one has been completed. Some may take the hybrid approach and read through the book working through some questions in the moment and coming back to others at a later time.

All of these approaches work.

You choose what style works best for you and how you learn and process.

You must also give yourself grace with your time allowance.

Some may read *The Connection Method* and complete the work in a week. While others may need to take their time and require three to four weeks to read and complete the process. Do what works for you, just don't give up! Keep doing the work!

The only wrong way is to not do it. You are guaranteed success if you don't give up. Keep reading, keep working and keep giving yourself grace no matter how you read, how you process, or how long it takes. You're here, that means you already are doing it "right."

RULE 2:
PERFECTIONISM IS OVERRATED + SHITTY ANSWERS ARE OK

The most authentic and honest Connection-Based Brands always start off as a disjointed brain dump, a messy word vomit, and a complete jumble of thoughts and ideas.

That's good. That's what you want.

One of my client's said that after she completed her answers to *The Connection Method*, she felt cathartic and like she was able to finally release all the things that had been swirling in her mind. She knew *The Connection Method* was a safe, non-judgmental, and confidential place, so she was able to let go, set aside perfectionism, be vulnerable, find clarity and step into her raw truth.

That's what I want for you too.

Trust your gut and don't over think your answers. Just write something.

If you try to have perfect answers that are manicured, flawless and try to please everyone, you will end up with a brand that is inauthentic and exhaustingly impossible to maintain.

In order to develop a genuine Connection-Based Brand, you have to embrace imperfect and own the real. But it first starts with some really imperfect, shitty answers.

RULE 3:
DON'T LET THE MONSTERS STOP YOU

Since you have now committed to giving yourself grace, throwing out perfection and allowing yourself to write those "shitty answers," I warn you that during this process, you may meet a couple nasty monsters along the way.

Most everyone encounters at least one (if not both) of them during this process, so I want you to be aware of them and know that it is completely "normal" to have one or both monsters pay you a visit every now and then. They are *The Current Mindset Monster* and *The Comparison Monster*.

MONSTER 1:
THE CURRENT MINDSET MONSTER

One of the biggest hurdles people encounter going through *The Connection Method* is fighting with their current perspective of themselves and business, aka the *Current Mindset Monster*.

We tend to get stuck thinking of ourselves as how we are now and where our business/leadership is at today versus having a forward-thinking perspective and seeing ourselves and our business in the future and having already "made it."

This is the mindset shift you need to have right now. Yes, right now, not a few pages from now, but right now, in this second.

As you go through this process, I want you to intentionally set your mindset as if you already are "successful" and have a business or position in leadership that you're proud of.

What does that look like?

Imagine it and operate and speak in that space as if you're already there.

Let that vision be your guide.

You may or may not currently have the thriving business or leadership position that you just imagined, but you already have the "goods." You already have the skills, or are on the path to gaining the skills you need to get there.

When I started writing this book, I repeatedly told myself, "I am an author. I wrote a book on Connection-Based Branding. My book helps entrepreneurs and leaders make an impact in their community. My book helps them stand confident in who they are what they offer."

I repeated this with full confidence, even though I only had a basic outline written and not much else. It was the "I'm already there" mindset and words I intentionally chose to speak in and think in, that were essential to push me, held me accountable and helped me write more pages in this book.

Being intentional with your mindset and the words you choose to say and think are the best way to combat the Current Mindset Monster so you can move past this monster and get to work on impacting your community with your Connection-Based Brand.

MONSTER 2:
THE COMPARISON MONSTER

The Comparison Monster is a beast that inserts its claws deep into your back, whispering words of insecurity in your ear like,

"Is there really a place for me?"

"Everyone else does this better than I do, why bother?"

"I feel like shit because I know I could never be like that person."

"Am I doing the right thing? Everyone else is doing something different."

"I will never measure up."

"I'm jealous."

"Everyone else is better than me."

"I'm worthless."

The Comparison Monster is a source of insecurity that has the power to instantly zap our confidence, and make us question our direction and self-worth. This monster also can take shape in other forms such as the I'm Not Good Enough Monster and the I'm Not Worthy Monster.

This nasty Monster appears in the quietest sectors of your brain, and if you allow it space, it completely takes over, causes havoc, prevents you from growing, and paralyzes your mind, body and business with fear and self-doubt.

The Comparison Monster most likely will pay a visit as you work though *The Connection Method*, so when it does, I am going to ask you to do one thing when it starts whispering things in your ear.

Acknowledge it.

Acknowledge the Comparison Monster's existence.

Speak to your Monster and say out loud, "Hey Comparison Monster! I just wanted to let you know that you're not allowed to drive my thoughts anymore. I acknowledge you're here, but please hop in the backseat. I need to drive my own car. I am busy creating something more important than the lies you're telling me."

Speak this statement out loud as you're going through the questions. This statement helps train your brain on how to deal with the Monster as it comes in and out of your mind. Once you have gone through *The Connection Method,* you can use your Connection-Based Brand as a shield against the Comparison Monster. Using the tangible elements of your Connection-Based Brand will combat the feeling of inadequacy or self-doubt.

Use the statement, and your developing Connection-Based Brand as your tool to fight the Comparison Monster. Don't let it halt your forward progression through the process.

RULE 4:
ESTABILISH YOUR WORK TOOL

As you embark on this process, I recommend establishing a work tool that will partner with you on this journey. There are *a lot* of questions you'll answer and process on the coming pages, so I recommend using a tool that works best for you and how you process/think. Maybe you think faster that you can write, so work on your computer and create special document file for your Connection Method notes.

If you like to write out your thoughts and doodling along the way helps you process, then I recommend buying a fresh notebook and pens for this process. Hopefully we will have an accompanying journal for this book soon, but in the meantime, find a tool that works for you and use it.

RULE 5:
FIND AN ACCOUNTABILITY PARTNER

If you want to get the most out of this process, I highly recommend partnering up with a friend and going through *The Connection Method* together! I suggest teaming up with a friend who you respect, who has the same or more motivation and drive as you do, who knows you, who is direct, who's not afraid to have tough conversations and can be a source of encouragement.

By having a standing accountability partner and timeline, you have just increased your chance of success by 95%. And spoiler alert ... I *really* want you to succeed!

Team up with an accountability partner and get to work!

"I WILL" STATEMENTS

As we wrap up this section and dive into the real work of *The Connection Method*, in addition to the rules, there is a list of I Will statements I want you to agree to.

Write them out in your chosen work tool (digital document or notebook) and keep these statements close to keep your brain and heart from wandering into insecurity and self-doubt while you work through the questions.

- ⇨ I will not overthink my answers.

- ⇨ I will write down my first instinct and will focus on what I truly want—even if it feels selfish, boastful, excluding, or too big of a dream.

- ⇨ I will not work for perfection, because imperfect answers are the best answers.

- ⇨ I will give myself permission speak highly of myself, even if it feels like bragging.

- ⇨ I will listen to and respect what my instincts/my gut is telling me.

- ⇨ I will not go back and overly edit my answers.

- ⇨ I will not hesitate to duplicate answers.

- ⇨ I will not rush through this process and I understand this takes time.

⇨   I will set up an ideal work environment when it's time to work.

⇨   … and most importantly … *I will not overthink my answers.*

Yes, that last "I Will" statement is intentionally repeated, because it is the most important one to remember during this process! Do not overthink, just answer. Shitty answers are welcomed and encouraged, remember?

BEFORE YOU START
Wrap Up

My last bit of advice before you head into *The Connection Method* process is this: take your time and know that you will get through it. This process is very in-depth and most likely very different from anything you have ever done before. It's meant to challenge you, your current mindset, and what you think you know about branding.

Being challenged is how we grow. If you experience struggle or difficulty along the way, just know it's a good sign. It means you are growing. It means you are challenging your status quo. It means you are digging deep, and that's when genuine connection with yourself can take root.

Now let's dive into what we all came here for … *The Connection Method*!

BEFORE YOU START

In this chapter you learned:

⇨ **The 5 rules of going through The Connection Method Process:**

1. Give yourself grace

2. Perfectionism is overrated + shitty answers are ok

3. Don't let the monsters stop you:

   - The Current Mindset Monster

   - The Comparison Monster

4. Establish your work tool

5. Find an accountability partner

⇨ **You read and agreed to the "I Will" statements**

CHAPTER FIVE

BRANDING WORDS

"People don't buy what you do, they buy why you do it."

- Simon Sinek, Author

If you only take away one thing from this book, let it be your Branding Words.

Your Branding Words are the most important element of The Connection Method and are the lifeblood and the foundation of your Connection-Based Brand. They are the starting point for everything else you define in the following chapters and will be the tool to help you stay consistent, validate decisions, and express your overall brand message.

Your Branding Words are your compass, your foundation, and your anchor to define who you are, what you value and what others can expect from you.

> " Branding Words are your compass, your foundation, and your anchor to define who you are, what you value and what others can expect from you. "

Once you have defined your Branding Words, you can firmly plant your feet, stand confidently and proclaim, "This is who I am! This is what I offer! This is me! Take it or leave it!"

The concept of Branding Words came to me back in 2010 when I started my photography business. Becoming a photographer was a decision made purely on instinct. My head, heart and intuition got together, had a board meeting and unanimously agreed that I needed to become a professional photographer.

The problem was, I didn't own a camera. I also didn't know how to operate it once I got a camera. I also had never owned a creative business before. The odds were stacked against me, but I went for it. I dove right in and started taking horrible photos. No, really, they were bad!

I had no idea what I was doing. I was insecure, my work was inconsistent, and I was completely lost. The only thing I was sure about was the fact that I was in the right place. Even though my work was kindergarten level, and perception of myself was less than ideal, I knew I was meant to be a photographer, so I kept at it.

As time went on, a familiar monster started showing up. Yep, the infamous Comparison Monster. This monster latched herself onto my back and started whispering insecurities and doubts into my ear.

As I watched other photographers on social media posting their beautiful work, I started second guessed who I was, and everything was doing. I wondered, "Should my photos be dark and moody or maybe light and airy?" "Maybe I need to shift my marketing systems and strategies?" "Their work turns out so much better than mine, why do I even bother?"

I was a prime target and extremely susceptible for the Comparison Monster's whispers because I was insecure, unconfident and scattered. I was all over the place, and lacked consistency. The clients I had didn't hire me on talent, but on faith, since they had no idea what to expect from me.

I was exhausted by it all. I knew that this was not the way to run a successful business or serve my clients long term, so something had to change. So, I sat myself down and had a real come-to-Jesus conversation with myself.

I started asking myself countless questions. Questions about who I was, what I wanted to be, who I wanted to serve, the type of art I wanted to create, and the type energy I wanted to give and attract. I even asked myself what type of perception I wanted others to have of me and my work and who I respected and didn't respect in my industry.

So. Many. Questions!

After processing my answers, I decided on four words that summarized all the answers I gave. I wanted my photography business, my work, my process, and the overall perception of me to be warm, real, timeless, and classic.

Warm, real, timeless and classic. Those four words became my first ever set of Branding Words. These are the words I built my photography business and grew my personal confidence.

I learned how to filter everything through my Branding Words, and I mean, everything. Such as how I conducted photoshoots, the type of photos I took, how I edited photos, opportunities, branding visuals and graphics, personal conversations, even down to what I wore. These four words helped me stay consistent. They helped me be intentional. They also became my shield against the Comparison Monster.

When I saw another photographer's work online and I started to feel less-than, I would stop and ask myself, "That is a beautiful photo, but is it warm, real, timeless and classic?"

Most of the time it wasn't. So, with that, I was able to acknowledge their work, and not let it affect me, my mindset or growth since it wasn't me, or MY brand. However, on the off chance it did align with my branding words, I would know which artists to pay more attention to and where I should glean intentional inspiration and education from. I let my Branding Words be my guide, filter and leader for everything I did, and still do it to this day.

As my business evolved past just photography and into branding education, speaking, writing, and community leadership, so have my Branding Words.

My current Branding Words are words that epitomize not only my work, but they are a direct reflection of me, my heart, my values, my mission and what my community (you) can expect from me.

My Branding Words are: real, education, inspiration, empower, and joy.

You may have already seen these words scattered throughout this book. You may have heard me speak them at an event, or seen them on social media. My Branding Words are synonyms with me, so my community knows exactly what to expect from me, how to perceive me and how to describe me.

That's the power of Branding Words. That's the clarity, consistency, confidence, and direction that await you once you define your Branding Words. They are the most important tool in your branding tool kit.

WHAT ARE BRANDING WORDS?

Branding Words are 3-5 words or phrases that define three key things:

 WHO you are

branding words
three to five words or phrases
defined by three key things

2 WHAT you value

3 WHAT OTHERS can expect from you

Branding Words are the anchor for your Connection-Based Brand. They define the character and purpose of your Connection-Based Brand, and they help you stay consistent, keep on track, and direct your growth. They act as filters for every decision you make. Decisions such as your website, logo, and business card design, how you market yourself, figuring out what opportunities to accept or decline, creating posts on social media, and even how you dress, interact with and speak to others. Everything you do will be a direct reflection of your Branding Words.

Branding Words also define the perception you want others to have about you and what you offer. Remember, you define how others perceive you and your brand, so it is vital to define intentional Branding Words and stay consistent within them.

Branding Words are also our grounding force when everything seems to be scattered and disconnected. We have all experienced it. When it feels like your business or career is going in 100 different directions and you don't know which way to go? Your Branding Words bring you back to center, ground you, and refocus your attention on your end goal, vision, and purpose.

Finding your words can take time, so give yourself grace as you identify these cores 3-5 words. Your words are allowed to change, grow and evolve over time, but you have to start somewhere. You must start here.

DEFINE YOUR BRANDING WORDS

BEFORE YOU PROCEED

If you are a solo entrepreneur or leader define your Branding Words for yourself. Go through the questions and focus on your goals, values, vision, and the experience you want to create for others.

If you are a part of a team, have each team member go through the questions on their own (make sure they focus on who they are and what they value as an individual—not just a resource to the team or the overall business).

Afterwards, have everyone come together for review. Take the Branding Words from each individual and find similarities.

When you are finished, everyone will have their own personal Branding Words, as well as an established set of core team/business Branding Words. It will look like a Venn diagram, with the core team/business

Branding Words in the middle and then each team member connected by their own circle. To remain consistent and have a shared vision, everyone must feel connected to the overall brand mission and vision.

STEP 1: THE BRANDING WORD QUESTIONS

Each category of questions is intended for you to connect with yourself. Remember, the truest form of connection comes from when others can see themselves in you, so this is the time for you to put in the hard work and define who you are.

These questions allow you to take the intangible thoughts and emotions you have swirling in your brain and turn them into something tangible; to define a real and intentional Connection-Based Brand.

The questions are vital to defining your brand and growing your business/career, so allow yourself time to go through them. Some of the questions might seem repetitive, but that is intentional. I've found that the more ways you look at something, the deeper you can go.

If you already have a good idea of your brand, these questions might take you an hour or two to complete. For others, it can take weeks from reading the question, processing it, and then answering.

Give yourself time and give yourself grace but give yourself a deadline to complete the questions. Don't forget to link up with your accountability partner to hold you to your schedule, or even go through the questions together.

Lastly, know that I have worded these questions as if you and I are having a one-on-one conversation, just like when I work with my one-on one clients. Thank you for bringing me along on this journey with you!

I don't take it lightly.

Now, grab your favorite drink, a yummy snack, your notebook or laptop, and cozy up, because it's time to dive into your Branding Word questions!

QUESTION SET 1 OF 3: THE BASICS

1. **On a scale of 1 to 10, how confident are you with your current brand?**

   (1= Not Confident - 10 = Extremely Confident)

2. **Why or why not do you feel confident with your current brand?**

   What specifically makes you confident or lack confidence?

3. **How would you describe your CURRENT brand?**

   If you don't know—what you are HOPING to create?

4. **What type of business or position do you hold?**
   - ○ Service based business
   - ○ Product based business
   - ○ Both service and product-based business
   - ○ Leader within an organization

5. **How would you describe YOUR role in the business or organization?**

   What product, service or skill do you provide?

QUESTION SET 2 OF 3: WHO YOU ARE

The biggest pitfall I see people going through these questions is to answer the questions just through their professional lens. Yes, filtering these questions through that lens is necessary, but don't forget that humans connect to humans, and need to see you for you, not just what you sell or offer. Don't forget to also process the questions through your personal lens as well.

1. **In a few short sentences, tell me how you got here—your personal story.**
   Share about your family, your background, where you grew up. Don't forget to include the painful parts of your story or unique things about you. Those are thing things that provide the deepest pieces of connection.

2. **In a few short sentences, summarize how you got to your current position in your business or leadership position?**
   Don't forget where you came from and all your hard work that got you here.

3. **What type of hobbies or activities to do enjoy OUTSIDE of work?**
   Consider activities such as recreation, travel, time with family, food + drink, movies + shows, build things, sports + athletics, etc. Note: you can share these types of activities on your website's

"about page" and can be illustrated in a Lifestyle Branding Photoshoot. A powerful connection piece.

4. **List a few words that you would use to describe your own personality?**

   Feel free to ask friends, family, coworkers, or clients for what words they would use to describe you! If you have a supportive community online, hop on social media and ask your friends and followers what words they would use to describe you!

5. **Think about your personal relationship(s) with your partner or close family and friends. What values and/or traits do you bring into these relationships?**

   Feel free to ask others if you don't know what you bring to the relationship.

6. **What values and/or traits does your partner or close family and friends have that you most appreciate?**

   TIP: After answering this, share your answer(s) with your partner and/or family and friends. It's a great way to show them that you care for and appreciate them!

7. **What brands or people inspire you?**

   Consider members of your family, businesspeople, celebrities, influencers, companies etc.

8. **Consider the above list of who you said inspires you. Why do these individuals or brands inspire you?**

   What about them makes you identify or connect with them?

9. **What words do you live by?**

Accountability	Innovation
Collaboration	Integrity
Commitment	Justice
Community	Kindness
Consistency	Leadership
Curiosity	Loyalty
Dependability	Open-Mindedness
Discipline	Optimism
Diversity	Passion
Education	Patience
Efficiency	Peace
Excellence	Perseverance
Faith	Positivity
Family	Quality
Freedom	Reliability
Honesty	Responsibility
Hope	Service

Teamwork   Trust

Transparency   Truth

QUESTION SET 3 OF 3: WHAT YOU VALUE

1. **Let's define what you value. From the list below, choose 3-5 words that best describe your personal core values.** Choose values that are rooted in who you are that you never depart from. Values that instinctually guide you on how to behave and treat others. What do you always fight for?

   If you have them, list any core value words that were not mentioned above.

2. **How do you want others to PERCEIVE, FEEL and SPEAK about you and/or your business?**
   Note: If you are a part of a team or larger company, please make two lists. 1) how you want others to perceive, feel and speak about YOU specifically as a leader, and 2) how you want others to perceive, feel and speak about the overall team/company.

3. **What makes you stand out in your industry? What makes you different?**
   It's ok to brag or speak proudly about yourself!
   Note: If you are a part of a team or larger company, please list 1) what makes YOU stand out and 2) what makes the overall team/ company stand out.

4. **What brands, businesses or people do you RESPECT?**

   Describe the characteristics of why you respect them.

5. **What brands, businesses or people do you NOT RESPECT?**

   Describe the characteristics of why you don't respect them.

6. **Would you consider yourself PROFESSIONAL in your business?**

   If so, describe the characteristics of HOW or WHY you are professional. What makes you "professional"?

7. **Would you consider yourself AUTHENTIC?**

   If so, what characteristics make you an authentic person or business? What makes you "authentic"?

WHAT OTHERS CAN EXPECT

One of the biggest fears people have is the fear of the unknown. If we clearly define and illustrate what your community can expect from you, they will feel more confident saying "yes" to what you have to offer.

Remember, when you have a clearly defined Connection-Based Brand, you define the narrative. You tell others what to expect from you and how to view you. The experience you provide is composed of three segments of time: *before* they meet/interact with you, *during* their interaction/work with you, and *after* their interaction/work with you.

The Before Experience: This is the span of time before they meet you, engage with you, hire you or purchase your product or service. This is the experience they have as they follow you on social media, during the referral process, learn about your story and/or research your offering online. This is the time when making that initial connection and making them feel seen, heard and matter is critical. You need to invest time and energy showing them what they can expect from you.

Crush their fear of the unknown by having a killer "about me" section on your website or resume, post behind the scenes photos and videos of you on social media, teach them something, show your personality, illustrate your process in whatever format you connect. When they can see who you are they will be more likely to reach out to connect directly.

The During Experience: Once your community has connected with you in the before experience and they feel like they know you and know what to expect, then the *during experience* can start.

The during experience is when they have decided to reach out for more information, want to connect or offer you an opportunity.

The during experience is when you and/or your team connect with them directly and offer them more information about your product, service, or leadership. At this stage, they have decided to directly engage and work with you and/or purchase your product/service.

In this stage, they are personally experiencing who you are and what you have to offer! They are personally experiencing your Connection-Based Brand.

The After Experience: This is the time after your work or project is done, your service has been provided and/or after they have been using your product for a while. Continuing the connection is vital so your direct community can transition into a referral source or "evangelist" for you and your brand.

BEFORE, DURING, AFTER QUESTIONS

1. **What type of experience do you want others to have with you/your business before meeting you/reaching out?**

   Think about when they view your social media or website or when someone talks about you. What do you want them to think or say about you before they meet you?

2. **What type of experience do you want others to have with you/your business during their actual interaction with you/your product?**

   Think about when you work with someone directly. How do you want their experience to feel or be carried out? How do you want them describing their experience with you to others?

3. **What type of experience do you want others to leave with after experiencing your product/service?**

   Think about when you have completed work with someone, how do you want them to speak about you to others. How do you want them to feel after working with you? How do you want to be remembered?

FIND YOUR PILOT LIGHT

In order to build the most genuine and authentic Connection-Based Brand, you have to know why, beyond monetary gain, you are doing what you are doing. There must be a deeper reason why you wake up and work hard. Some people call this your Why. I call it your personal pilot light.

A pilot light is a small flame which powers things like your heater or fireplace. The pilot light stays on all the time and flickers at the ready to ignite a larger fire.

My pilot light, the thing that drives me is when I can inspire others to feel seen, heard and know that they matter. When I follow my pilot light, it causes a ripple effect enacting change and greater impact beyond me. That's what drives me is to help empower my community to learn that they truly matter. That their voice matters, and needs to be heard. That they are not alone and are in this together. That is my pilot light. That is what drives me.

Now it's time to find yours.

1. **What motivates you to do what you do?**

   Is it inspiring others, helping people find a solution, creating global or local impact? Is it putting a roof over your family's head? What is it?

2. **Why are you building this business or are in your current leadership position? Why is this important to you?**

   Give yourself some time with this one. Go on a walk, have a coffee conversation with a friend. Dig deep. Why the hell are you working so hard to build this specific business or career?

THAT'S IT!

Hooray! Your Branding Word Questions are done! You slayyyyyyyyed it! Snaps all around! Now, let's take your answers and define your 3-5 Branding Words!

Before you proceed though, I have a hot tip for you!!

Please remember these two words: simplify and summarize. Keep it simple and choose words that summarize the overall value, feeling or experience you want to portray.

STEP 2: PICK YOUR WORDS

When picking your words, comb through your answers and look for two things:

1. **Find repetitive words.** Highlight them and compile a list of those repetitive/common words.

2. **Find common phrases or themes**. Look at the overarching theme of what you are saying.

For example, if you wrote: "It's really important to me that my clients feel like they can trust me because I am always honest with them" then you can pull the words "trust" and "honest" since that is what you value.

STEP 3: LOOK BACK

Look back at your answers to the questions, take note, and write down repeated or similar words and phrases, and/or words and phrases that excite you, that mirror who you truly are and the experience you want to offer.

Feel free to write down any additional words or phrases that define who you are and what you offer (see the Branding Words list for inspiration).

This is the place for you to go word crazy! Write them all down!

STEP 4: THE BRANDING WORDS LIST

The following list of words are suggestions that can encapsulate multiple words and values into one. You can use words from this list or pick your own unique words. This list acts as a tool to provide inspiration and to help you narrow down your words.

Note: Branding Words with an * next to them means they are the most popular, most used words among our Connection Crew. Please don't shy away from using a "popular" word. They are well used for a reason! These words summarize overarching personal values and brand messages well! Even if you share a Branding Word with someone else, you will live it out and implement it completely differently than they will!

Accessible

Adventurous

Advisor*

Ambitious

Approachable

Body-Positive

Bold

Calm

Care

Casual

Clarity

Classic

Classy

Clean

Clever

Comfortable

Commitment

Communication*

Community*

Compassion

Confidence

Connection*

Conservative

Contemporary

Consistent

Courage

Craft

Creative

Custom

Culture

Dedicated

Dependable

Diligent

Direct

Dramatic

Edgy

Education*

Elegant

Empathy

Empower*

Energetic

Energy

Excellence*

Exclusive

Experienced*

Feminine

Fresh

Friendly

Fun

Funky

Fun-Loving

Genuine

Glamorous

Goal-Driven

Grounded

Health/Healthy

Helpful

Honest

Humorous

Imaginative

Innovative*

Inspiration/Inspire*

Instinctual

Integrity*

Intuitive

Joy/Joyful

Leader*

Leadership

Loyal

Luxurious/Luxury

Magnetic

Masculine

Maverick

Mysterious

Non-Judgmental

Original

Passion

Peace

Polished*

Positive

Powerhouse

Precise

Proactive

Quirky

Radiance

Real*

Rebellious/Rebel

Refined

Relatable

Relationships

Relaxed

Resilient

Resource*

Retro

Rugged

Safe-Haven

Simple

Solutions*

Southern

Spiritual

Steady

Tenacious

Timeless

Tough

Traditional

Transparency

Trust*

Trustworthy

Unique

Vigilante

Warm

Welcoming

Witty

STEP 5: SUMMARIZE YOUR WORDS

Now it's time to keep only the words that summarize who you are and resonate with you the most. Choose words that describe the essence of you, words that you don't have to try to be. Choose words that unconsciously radiate from you.

Do not choose words that you have to work towards or that you aspire to be. Choose words that come naturally to you. Choose words that you feel good about and inspire some sort of emotional reaction.

While summarizing your words, think about words that define who you are and what you value, but also don't forget to shift the spotlight to your community as well. Find words that reflect what type of experience others can expect. Think about the energy you put out, your personality, your sense of humor, your service experience, your product experience, your leadership experience, your process. What can they expect?

STEP 6: DEFINE YOUR WORDS

Look at the words you just identified and make a list of **only the top 3-5 words** that summarize and encapsulate who you are, what you value and what people can expect from you.

It is vital to limit your Branding Words to a maximum of 5. You want to keep things simple and be able to remember and speak your Branding Words as easy as you say your coffee order!

If you are having a hard time summarizing, or need help knowing how similar words relate to each other, check out the information below on Word Sets and Sub-Words. There is also a section on Team Words if you are a part of a larger group/business.

WORD SETS: Not everyone has a word set, but if it makes sense for you, a Branding Word can be two words put together. When you do this, that is called a Word Set.

A Word Set is when you combine two words in order to specifically define the type of word you are describing. For example, an artist may choose Simple Elegance because their work and experience aren't just simple or just elegant, but a combination of the two. Another example is Edgy Fun. A leader may choose Edgy Fun because her sense of humor and personality has a more edgy vibe to it versus a warm, fuzzy, sunshine, and rainbows fun.

I recommend using Word Sets sparingly since the goal is to simplify and summarize. However, if you must use a Word Set, only allow one or two sets in your overall Branding Word list.

SUB-WORDS: After you have gone through and defined your core Branding Words, I am sure there will be words left over but are still important to you. This is where Sub-Words come into play.

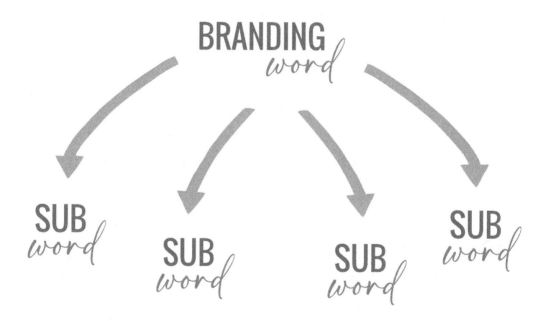

Sub-Words support a main Branding Word. For example, if one of your core Branding Words is *Integrity*, you may have Sub-Words such as trust, honesty, or ethical. Integrity is the main umbrella Branding Word that summarizes and represents all the Sub-Words.

Sub-Words are supportive words that uplift your main Branding Word. Another example is if one of your core Branding Words is *Support*, you can have Sub-Words such as transparency, collaboration, and leader. These Words are how you individually provide and carry out support for your community.

TEAM WORDS: As I mentioned at the beginning of this section, if you are a part of a team or group of leaders working together, have each of you go through the questions and steps on your own. Once you each have a set of your 3-5 Branding Words, bring your Words together.

Look at your Words and look for overlap. Look for common Words and themes that the team shares together.

Take those shared Branding Words and place them in the middle of a Venn diagram. Then take each team members words and put them in the outer circles. This forms your Team Branding Word Diagram reflecting your team's core values as well as the unique values each person individually brings to the table.

Team Branding Word Diagram can look as simple as this ...

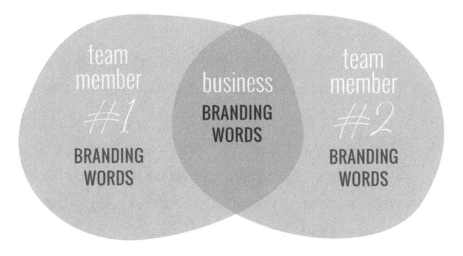

Or it can look more complex when you have more people involved.

STEP 7: FEEL THE FEELS

Take stock of the 3-5 Branding Words you just defined in Step 6, as well as any Word Sets or Sub-Words you may have defined. How do they feel?

Do they represent you and your experience? Do they represent how you want others to see you? Is this how you want to run your business or how you operate as a leader? Do you feel confident having these words/phrases represent you and what you offer?

Go through the following questions and check if the words you chose clearly represent what Branding Words are:

⇨ Do they describe who you are?

⇨ Do they describe what you value?

⇨ Do they describe what others can expect from you?

If you answered "yes," to those three questions, and you feel confident in your Branding Words, then move to Step 8!

If you answered "no", and you're second guessing your words and your gut is telling you these words don't represent you, I would suggest you go through the following sub steps: 1) put away your words, 2) go through the questions again, and 3) move forward.

SUB STEP 7.1: PUT YOUR WORDS AWAY

If you are struggling with your Branding Words and overthinking them, put your words away for a week.

As you take a break from your words, I want you to listen to the words around you. What you say about yourself. What others say about you. Listen and absorb. When you come back to your words, see if they align with how you speak about yourself and how others perceive you/your experience. Do they align or do they need to be adjusted?

SUB STEP 7.2: GO BACK THROUGH

If your words are *still* feeling off, go back through the questions and make sure you provide the most honest and genuine answers. If you are not being honest with your answers, then your Branding Words will reflect that inauthenticity and they won't feel "right" in your gut.

SUB STEP 7.3: MOVE FORWARD

If you still feel stuck, or are experiencing Olympic level overthinking, go ahead and move forward with the words you have. Remember, Branding Words can change and evolve as you grow and develop over time, but you have to start somewhere. Start to use and integrate the words you have and allow yourself flexibility to change them as you grow.

STEP 8: DEFINE YOUR CORE WORD

I am so excited and so proud of you! You have defined your 3-5 Branding Words! This is no small feat, and these words are going to be the foundation for everything you do moving forward in *The Connection Method* and out in the real world. Way to go!

Before we move on, I want to give you an opportunity to dig a little deeper with your words by defining your Core Branding Word.

Look at your 3-5 words and think about the one word that represents you and your mission to the core! Think about the word that summarizes you best. Think about if all the other words disappeared and you were just left with one word, which one would it be?

This word is your Core Word. It sits at the top of your Branding Word List. It will be underlined and bold. This word is the captain of your proverbial Connection-Based Brand ship. It will be the first thing you always come back to when making decisions in your business or career.

For example, my Branding Words are: *Real, Education, Inspiration, Empower* and *Joy*. All of my words are extremely important, but in the end, if all my other words were to disappear, I will always be *Real* with people, no matter what. I will connect and communicate with them and show up as my *Real* self.

Defining your Core Word simplifies the filtering process even further by having one word you always come back to.

What is your Core Word?

STEP 9: WORKSHOP YOUR BRANDING WORDS

Workshopping your Connection-Based Brand is always my favorite step in *The Connection Method* process. Why? Because it involves food, drinks, and friends.

In this step, you need to invite your best friend or a group of trusted friends over or go out to eat.

This time is for you to take your new Branding Words out for a trial run out in the real world. It is important though, to not invite your "yes friends," the ones who just say "yes" to everything and don't have an opinion of their own. Invite 1-3 friends who you respect, who are not afraid to give their opinion, who can ask you challenging questions.

Once you sit down at the table and are ready to discuss, start off the conversation with ...

"I am about to share with you my Branding Words. These Words not only represent what I do in my business or career, but they also reflect who I am as a person and what type of experience people can expect when working with me or even being my friend.

Once I share my Branding Words, I ask that you are truthful but kind since I have worked really hard at putting these Words together. I am sharing these words with you to validate that I am heading in the right direction, and if not, I am open to honest discussion about changes or ideas. Are we all on the same page?"

Then share your Branding Words. Ask if they feel your words reflect who you are. If you feel passionate about a word and they challenge it, fight for your word. This exercise is for you to get your legs under you and to bring your Branding Words out from being contained in your mind, into the real world. These conversations validate your Word choice and reassure you that you are going in the right direction when you start to second guess yourself.

Once you have discussed, workshopped, and made tweaks to your Branding Words, now it's time to own and use them!

STEP 10: OWN + USE YOUR WORDS

The final step in the Branding Word process is to *own your words.* These words are the foundation element of everything we do moving forward in *The Connection Method.* They are also your compass for how you portray yourself/your Connection-Based Brand and make consistent and confident decisions out in the real world.

In order to own your words, you need to get really intimate with them. Hop into bed with them and cuddle up, because they are going to be your best friend and partner as you move forward not only through *The Connection Method*, but also as you grow your business and leadership! So, snuggle up!

The best way to get "intimate" with your words is to always have them in front of you. I have mine printed and framed in my house and as my desktop background! You can also put them on a Post-It™ note by your computer, on your fridge or your steering wheel. You can even make them your background on your cell phone. Always have your Branding Words near you so you can repeat them and memorize them, so they can start to become second nature to you.

As you start to own your words, you can simultaneously start using them in the real world! Describe yourself and what you have to offer through these words. Start practicing filtering decisions, thoughts, and ideas through your words, and start speaking these words to your community. You will also use your Branding Words to define the rest of your Connection-Based Brand in the coming chapters, so have them handy!

BRANDING WORDS
Wrap Up

I hate to sound like a broken record, but it's worth repeating. What you've just defined in this chapter, your Branding Words, is the most important part of your Connection-Based Brand. You will use these Words to direct and filter everything else you create moving forward.

However, even though they are incredibly vital to the development of your brand, I don't want you overthinking or second guessing what you have defined as your Words. What you have defined is good enough. In fact, the Words you have defined are more than good enough, even if you feel insecure or have doubts.

Using and implementing your Branding Words is a learned skill that takes time and practice. At first, you will probably look and feel like a baby giraffe learning to walk for the first time, stumbling, falling, tripping, and second guessing your next steps. But don't fight your Branding Words, let them guide you.

As you grow and start walking more confidently with them, your Branding Words will grow and evolve with you. They change as you change or even stay the same, but you have to start somewhere. You have to start here and commit to your words. They are more than good enough.

BRANDING WORDS

In this chapter you learned:

⇨ What are Branding Words

⇨ The Branding Word questions

⇨ How to define your Branding Words

⇨ Word-Sets and Sub-Words

⇨ How to own and use your Branding Words

⇨ To share your Branding Words with The Connection Crew on social media with #MyBrandingWords and #TheConnectionMethod

CHAPTER SIX

IDEAL COMMUNITY

"Stick with people who pull the magic out of you,
not the madness."

-*UNKOWN*

I know what you must be thinking, "Ummm, Kels, what's this Ideal Community idea? Don't you mean ideal client?"

Well, remember, my friend, Connection-Based Branding is about challenging the status quo and flipping traditional branding upside down in order to look at it from a new perspective. So, the concept of an "ideal client" is no different. We are going to look at who you want to attract from a different perspective as well.

Instead of an Ideal Client, I want you to define your Ideal Community.

Traditionally, when you focus on defining just your ideal client, it creates a linear and *transaction-based relationship*. You are focusing on sales instead of connection.

On the flip side, an Ideal Community is not solely focused on the end transaction. Instead, an Ideal Community takes a broader, more encompassing view of those you want to attract. It focuses on defining the overall characteristics of different types of people you want to bring into your larger Community—not just who buys from you. Your Ideal Community is characteristics-based not just transaction-based.

Your Ideal Community looks at your bigger circle and not only includes individuals or opportunities that give you money, jobs, and clients, but it also includes your team, leadership, friends and family. Your Ideal Community comes from being intentional about those you want to attract, engage with, serve, lead, and support in your life and business. It's about focusing on the characteristics, values, qualities, and personalities of the people you want to attract *first* and then specific demographics.

WHAT IS AN IDEAL COMMUNITY?

Your Ideal Community is an individual or group who you serve or are being served by. They are the people who support you and uplift you towards your goals. Instead of traditional branding where you first focus on defining a specific demographic or ideal client avatar, with your Ideal Community, you define the specific type of characteristics of the individuals you most want to attract to your overall Community.

If you focus solely on seeing people as statistics and attracting a certain demographic, say for example, stay-at-home moms, aged 25-45, in the greater Seattle area, looking to make extra money on the side, your focus will be concentrated on those details. That's all well and good, until you attract someone like this, but their characteristics, energy, values, and personality don't align with yours. They may match your demographic perfectly, but if your values don't align, it will deplete your energy, stall your growth, and take away time you could be giving to individuals who align with your values.

People are like ducks on a pond, if you start feeding one, more show up wanting what you have to give. It's important to feed the healthy and appreciative ducks vs the toxic and entitled ducks. If you feed the healthy ducks, more will show up like them. If you feed the toxic ducks, more will show up like them. It's ducking logic.

The types of people you serve and the people who serve you are directly linked to not only your success in your business or career, but also to the well-being of your mental, emotional, and physical health. So, it's vital to be explicitly intentional with who you allow into your circle.

One of my clients said that after she defined her Ideal Community, she had the tools to clearly identify those she was excited to work with, the people who would appreciate and trust her. She was also able to identify the people who would be damaging to her mental health and confidence.

She took her scattered emotions and questions of, "Who should I work with?"

"Who should I say no to and why?"

"Who should I allow to lead me?"

"I'm afraid of hurting people's feelings if I say no to them," and turned them into a clearly defined, tangible Ideal Community. She defined a clear list of who she was energized by and who she was drained by. She was able to decisively filter not only her clients but also team members, personal leadership as well as the personal relationships through her Ideal Community. She was empowered to know why she was saying yes to some and saying no to others.

Defining your Ideal Community gives you the power, validation, and confidence to be known for exactly who you want to intentionally attract to your Community as well as know exactly who you want to repel from your Community and why.

The roles in your Ideal Community should not be given easily. They should be curated so you attract and surround yourself with exactly the type of people who energize you, support you, believe in you, and who push you to keep going.

You connect most with people like you, so you want to attract people like you. You want to attract people with similar values, characteristics, personality, sense of humor, backgrounds, interests, and areas where they need to serve.

You define who you allow into your Community. You are the one who has the key to attract the ideal and repel the less-than-ideal.

"You define who you allow into your Community. You are the one who has the key to attract the ideal and repel the less-than-ideal."

There are four different groups within your Ideal Community. Each represents an individual or group who has the power to support your goals and vision or devalue your goals and vison by wasting your precious time, energy, and financial resources.

These four groups of your Ideal Community are your:

⇨   Ideal Client

⇨   Ideal Team

⇨   Ideal Leadership

⇨   Ideal Support Crew

As you define your Ideal Community, keep in mind that the characteristics you want to attract will, in general, be applicable to all four roles. Similarly, the characteristics and values you want to repel will also be applicable to all four roles.

THE 4 GROUPS OF AN IDEAL COMMUNITY

1. IDEAL CLIENT

Yes, you do have an Ideal Client.

Whether you are an entrepreneur or a leader within an organization, you have some sort of Ideal Client represented in your Community. For entrepreneurs, this is someone who you specifically market to and who will purchase your product or service.

If you are a leader within an organization, your Ideal Client could be your employer, the company, or contractor who hires you to do a job. Your Ideal Client is based on who your work is directly serving.

2. IDEAL TEAM

Ideal Team is composed of individuals or teams of people who help you run your business and/or help you do your job. They can be employees, contractors, colleagues, team members or support staff. Your Ideal Team plays a vital role as the backbone to support you and help you reach your goals.

If you are in the beginning stages of your business or career, the idea of having an Ideal Team may feel out of reach. However, I urge you to start prepping yourself to receive help even in the smallest ways. The greatest advice I have ever been given is, "True growth can only happen when you are willing to ask for and receive help from others."

Prep yourself now. Start dreaming and visualizing the type of people you want in your corner as your Ideal Team, so when they do show up, you can identify them immediately and team up without hesitation!

3. IDEAL LEADERSHIP

One of the most draining side effects of being a leader is that you are expected to always give, give, give. Unless you are intentional about bringing balance, it seems like leaders are always giving and rarely given back to in return. We find ourselves pouring so much into others, that unless we have someone (or something) pouring back into us, our energy bucket eventually dries up.

In order to avoid feeling like an unbalanced scale of support for others, you must identify the characteristics of your Ideal Leadership. Define what type of characteristics you want leading you. Define the kind of leadership that will show up for you and help replenish, inspire, revive, and energize you so you can keep serving others.

An Ideal Leader is not always a one-on-one relationship. An Ideal Leader can be an individual or it can be a resource which aids your growth as a leader.

The Ideal Leadership role can be composed of mentors, corporate leadership, educators, spiritual leaders, authors, public figures, speakers, etc. Ideal Leadership can appear in the form of one-on-one interactions or even resources such as a podcasts, books, blogs, social medias, videos, conferences, or online courses.

No matter what Leadership source you attract and integrate, it is vital that their vision, message, values, and energy aligns with your overall Ideal Community characteristics.

4. IDEAL SUPPORT CREW

Your Ideal Support Crew is composed of your closest family and friends. Those who just "get you" and have a desire to see you succeed. They withhold judgment but provide constructive criticism, encouragement, support, and wisdom as you navigate the business ownership and/or leadership waters. They are the ones you go to for rest, venting, and celebration. They are your sounding board and the ones who keep you grounded as your success and impact grows. They are essential and non-negotiable. They are your Ideal Support Crew.

You must remember that you are more than an asset, a paycheck, or a resource. You are a human. A human with emotions, fears, excitement, and big goals and dreams that need to be carefully supported and nurtured. Your Ideal Support Crew is here to bring that level of human support. They know you as you, not your job description and can support you in a real way.

If you don't currently have a Support Crew behind you or are surrounded by negative family and friends, it's going to be an Everest-like climb to the top. If this is you, after you define your Ideal Community, your mission is to seek out a Support Crew that aligns with your Ideal Community characteristics, and will be a positive source of support in your life. This is priority number one.

THE "WHAT IF" FEAR MONSTER

Before you dive into the nitty-gritty of defining the specific characteristics of who your Ideal Community is, I want to address the What If Fear Monsters that may invite themselves to the I'm-defining-my-kickass-Ideal-Community party.

The What If Fear Monster may creep into the back of your mind and whisper, "... if I only attract these types of people, what about the other people?" or "What if I make others feel left out?" or "What if I miss an opportunity because I am laser-focused on attracting this type of person?" or "Oh, god! What if, what if, what if?!"

I address this specific monster because I personally have experienced it as well as almost every one of my clients. Be forewarned that people pleasers and those who say yes to everyone for fear of hurting their feelings are the most susceptible to the What If Fear Monster's whispers and lies. I know, because I'm one of them.

After a childhood of being bullied and left out of activities and events, I ride the struggle bus with people pleasing and try to make sure everyone feels included. I don't like the feeling of being left out, so I don't want others to feel the same. I've made it my personal mission to make sure others never feel that way. If I'm at a party, I seek out individuals who are sitting alone and sit next to them. When I'm in a group, I try to connect with as many people as possible. I honestly believe that this is where my passion for seeking out and creating genuine connections comes from. However, I know too well that if you attempt to serve everyone, I guarantee you will burn out, overworked, overwhelmed, taken advantage of, and serving people who do not energize or support your overall mission.

Another common prey for to the What If Fear Monster to attach to are individuals who have a scarcity mindset. Those who are afraid if they only focus on serving a specific type or group of people, that their business or career will suffer monetarily, or lack opportunity. I promise you; this is not the case. There is plenty, in fact, more than enough business and growth opportunities waiting for you within your Ideal Community circle.

" There is plenty, in fact, more than enough business and growth opportunities waiting for you within your Ideal Community circle. "

Did you read that? There is more-than-enough.

If you are in a constant cycle of grasping at straws, saying yes to everything and everyone, and running your life, business, and career out of fear that there will never be enough, you will never receive enough and you will attract never enough. You will attract scarcity minded people who will drain you and take advantage of you since you will never be enough to them. What you put out will come back.

To shift that focus, you must be willing to define your Ideal Community and fully commit to attracting and serving only them. Your Ideal Community wants the best for you, so let's honor them by giving them our time energy and resources, not the ones who drain us. Let's shut the door on the What If Fear Monster's face, because they're not welcome to this party.

DEFINE YOUR IDEAL COMMUNITY: THE QUESTIONS

The following questions are meant to help you define the specific characteristics and values of your Ideal Community. As you go through the next section, do not let the What If Fear Monster block your mind or your answers. Go with your gut and remember to go for good-enough, not perfect, because shitty answers are ok!

Pretend all the external noise, expectations and pressure is gone, and imagine that you get to hand pick your absolute favorite people to work with, serve and receive support (because you do!). Focus on the people who energize you, not deplete you. Focus on the people who appreciate and respect the work that you do not the ones who take advantage of you. Focus on the people you want 100 more of in your life because those are the people you are focused on defining and attracting.

IF YOU ARE JUST STARTING OUT

If you are just starting out and are at the beginning of your business or career, you may not know who you love working with yet. How are you supposed to know who you love working with and who you want to attract to your Community if you're just starting out?

The answer: focus on your personal experiences.

Personally, you have experienced people who you love spending time with and those you don't. You have experienced people who energize you and those who deplete you. You have experienced people who respect you and those who don't. Use those individuals as your inspiration for your Ideal Community as you move through the questions.

QUESTION SET 1 OF 2: EVALUATE

1. **On a scale of 1 to 10, how confident are you with describing, knowing, or attracting exactly who you want to attract to your circle?**

   1: Not Confident - 10: Extremely Confident

2. **Do you find yourself saying yes to every client, customer, person, or opportunity that comes along? Or are you very specific with who you work with, sell to or invite into your overall circle?**

   ○ Say yes to everyone

   ○ Somewhere in the middle

   ○ Very specific and focused with who I attract

3. **What percentage of your CURRENT community are composed of people who ENERGIZE you?**

   ○ 80%-100%

   ○ 60%-70%

   ○ 50%

   ○ 30%-40%

   ○ Below 20%

4. **What percentage of your CURRENT community are composed of people who DEPLETE you?**

   ○ 80%-100%

   ○ 60%-70%

   ○ 50%

   ○ 30%-40%

   ○ Below 20%

5. **On a scale of 1 to 10, how much of a people pleaser are you?**

   1: Not a people pleaser - 10: Extreme people pleaser (can't say no)

QUESTION SET 2 OF 2: CHARACTERISTICS

In the following questions, think about your *favorite* person or people. This person(s) can be a client, team member, a leader, a supportive person in your life or even a public figure. Think about the person(s) who energize you. Think about the person you respect and who respects you. Think about the person(s) you wish you had 10 or even 100 more of in your life and/or business. Got this person in mind? Great, use them as your inspiration and source to answer the following questions.

1. **Think about your *favorite* person, describe the characteristics of why they are your favorite.**
   Describe their personality, values, behavior/actions, or any unique characteristics (or quirks) you appreciate most about them.

2. **Think about this *favorite* person (or people), does this person energize you? If so, explain what about them energizes you and motivates you to want to go the extra mile for them.**
   Write down specific characteristics or behaviors they possess that energize you.

3. **Think about how your *favorite* people describe you and perceive you. What characteristics do you have that others connect with most? What elements of themselves do they see in you?**
   Think about your Branding Words and how others describe you. What personal characteristics of yours do others connect with and cling to most?

4. **Why do your *favorite* people respect you?**
   Think about the things they appreciate about you, the characteristics that make you unique to them. What personal characteristics do you possess that others respect?

5. **In your personal life and relationships, think about the person(s) you trust, admire and respect. Describe the characteristics of this person and why you respect them**.
   If applicable, it can be the same person you consider to be your "favorite" person. Is it experience? Personality? Job description? Their values? Career evolution? Overall energy and vibe? Their personal story? What draws you to them? Write down specific characteristics or behaviors they possess that make you respect them.

6. **Think of brands, businesses, influencers, or public figures who you respect, why do you respect them?**
   Is it experience? Their product? Personality? Their values? What they teach? Their aesthetic? Career evolution? Overall energy and vibe? Their personal story? What draws you to them? Write down specific characteristics or behaviors they possess that make you respect them.

7. **Think about the person or brand/business you just described in the previous two questions. What elements of yourself do you see in this person and/or brand? What**

are the connection pieces that tie you two together?
Is it that you share similar backstories and struggles? Is it your demographic (age, sex, location?)? Do you look like them? How are they a reflection of who you are or who you what you want to be?

8. **What is the *one value* you hold true to and expect your Community to be committed to upholding as well? What is one value that is nonnegotiable?**
    Is it integrity, truth, loyalty, respect, compassion, community, empathy, hard work, open mindedness, social justice, dependability, freedom, etc? If you need to, refer to the Glossary of Terms in the back of the book for a full list of core value examples.

Now, let's look at the flipside of the previous questions. Think about your *least favorite* person. This person(s) can be a client, team member, a leader, negative person in your life or even a public figure. Think about the person(s) who deplete you. Think about the person(s) you don't respect and who doesn't respect you. Think about the person(s) you don't enjoy working with or being around.

I know this section can feel uncomfortable, because we never want to "talk bad" about others, but you must define both sides. You must be clear on not only who you want to attract (who energizes you), but also who you want to repel (who depletes you). No one will see your answers except you, so please be honest. Use your least favorite person as your source to answer the following questions. Write down specific characteristics or behaviors they exhibit that make them your least favorite.

1. **Think about your *least favorite* person, describe the characteristics of why they are your *least favorite*.**
   Describe their personality, values, behavior/actions, or any unique characteristics or quirks you don't appreciate about them.

2. **Think about this *least favorite* person (or people), does this person deplete your energy? If so, explain what about them exhausts you.**
   Write down specific characteristics or behaviors they possess that deplete you.

3. **In your personal life and relationships, think about the person(s) you don't trust, don't admire, and don't respect. Describe the characteristics of this person and why you do not respect them**.
   If applicable, it can be the same person you consider to be your "least favorite" person. Is it their energy and overall vibe? Is it their negative speak and mindset? Is it their disregard for others? Is it their personal story? Is it their lack of respect? Is it their jealously? Write down specific characteristics or behaviors they possess that make you not respect them.

4. **Think of brands, businesses, influencers, or public figures who you don't respect, why don't you respect them?**

Is it their work ethic and systems? Is it their lack of social awareness? Their personality? Their values, or lack of values? Their aesthetic? Overall energy and vibe? Their personal story? Write down specific characteristics or behaviors they possess that make you not respect them.

5. **Think about the person or brand/business you just described in the previous two questions. Are there any negative behaviors or characteristics they have that you've adopted for yourself? Are there any undesirable connection pieces that tie you two together?**
We are a direct reflection of who we surround ourselves with, so if we are subconsciously adopting negative behaviors and characteristics from those we don't respect, that has to change now! Sometimes we don't know something is a problem until it's pointed out. This is the question for you to be honest with yourself to see if there are any negative characteristics you have taken on so you can start the process of getting rid of them A.S.A.P.

CREATE YOUR ATTRACT + REPEL LISTS

Now it's time to go through all your answers from the previous questions and condense them into two tangible lists: your Attract List and your Repel List. Your Attract List is a specific summary of the 5-10 core characteristics you want to attract to your Ideal Community. Your Repel List is a specific summary of the 5-10 characteristics you want to repel from your Ideal Community.

These two lists help you tangibly define those you want to attract and those you need to repel. Remember that it's ok, in fact, necessary for you to repel people. Repel is a strong and spikey word, and I use it for a reason. Repel it is exactly what you need to do to the people who do not align with your values and energy. Intentionally repelling specific people is not rejecting them, but instead an act of respect that honors your Ideal Community.

> " Intentionally repelling specific people is not rejecting them, but instead an act of respect that honors your Ideal Community. "

These two lists will be the tools you use to filter people. They will help you decide if someone is a good fit for you and will add to your Community or if they will distract and diminish your Community. If you are getting an "off" vibe from someone, go back to your Attract and Repel Lists. Most of the time that "off" vibe is your intuition telling you that they are Repel Listers and don't align with your Ideal Community characteristics. The opposite is true as well. If you are getting a "positive and connected" vibe from someone, this person probably has characteristics directly correlated to your Attract List.

Whether you feel off about someone or you feel a kinship with someone, go back to your lists. You'll be able to identify exactly why you two connect, or don't connect. Your Attract and Repel Lists are here to turn the emotional vibes and your intuition about others into a tangible list. These lists allows you to know why someone would be a good fit as well as why someone wouldn't be a good fit.

The best illustration I have about the Repel List comes from one of my incredible clients, Monica, who immigrated to the United States from Italy.

When she came to the United States, she didn't know anyone. She learned English from scratch, and had to adopt a new culture, and a new way of life. Despite the hardships, she built a successful business and loyal Community. A truly incredible woman.

As we went through *The Connection Meth*od together and I brought up her Repel List, Monica read the word *repel* and looked confused. Since English was her second language, she had explained to me that certain words sometimes needed further explanation.

She focused on the word *repel* then looked at me and in her beautiful, thick, Italian accent, with rolling r's she asked, "Repel, like..." She held her hand up as if holding an imaginary aerosol can and pretended to spray the air "Pssst-pssst. Like a spray to repel all the bugs?"

After we laughed together at her bug spray pantomime, I confirmed, "Yes! That was exactly it!"

Your Repel List is intended to, just like a bug spray repellent, spray away anyone who doesn't respect you, doesn't value you, drains your energy, and isn't a source of positive energy. You need to know exactly the characteristics of the people you want to repel, so when you encounter them, you know when to "Pssst-pssst" spray your repellent and walk away, because they are not for you!

I remember when I had to fire my first client. In our initial conversations, it seemed as if her values aligned perfectly with my Attract List, so I took her on. However, as time went on, her true character came out.

She was not willing to commit to do the work, and she blatantly disrespected me and my time. I kept giving her chances and opportunities to show up, but I was consistently met with excuses and disrespect of my time. When I gave her one more chance, and she failed to show up, that was it. I knew I had to end the relationship.

Even though I was frustrated, hurt, and disrespected, I didn't want to base my decision to end our relationship purely on my frustrated emotions. I went back to my Repel List (which I should have done earlier when the bad vibes started appearing) and cross checked the list with her behavior and treatment of me.

You know what I discovered? She hit over 90% of the characteristics of my Repel List. She had bad energy, was disrespectful, was focused on transactions not connection, not looking to learn, was arrogant, was superficial, couldn't see the bigger picture, was not committed to the work, and lead with excuses.

My Repel List confirmed my gut feelings. I had my confirmation. My Repel List provided me the tangible reasons for why we were not a good fit and could no longer work together.

In my email to her (yes, you must communicate and not avoid), I didn't speak from emotion saying "I'm mad at you and I don't like you." No, because of my tangible Repel List, I was able to clearly spell out that our business values didn't align and that I wasn't a good fit for her to help her achieve her goals. I sent her a recommendation for someone else and wished her the best. After I hit send, I instantly felt a sense of peace and relief letting her go, and I knew I made the right choice.

Because I let her go, I was able to give my time, energy, and resources to someone from my Attract List. An Attract Lister who valued, respected, and appreciated my time, talents, and what I have to offer. Once you start saying no to your Repel Listers, your time and energy can now be freely given to your Attract Listers.

Both your Attract and Repel Lists are powerful tools which help you move from making purely emotional decisions, to being able to make intentional decisions.

Your Attract and Repel Lists are a partner to your Branding Words. They will be extremely helpful to my people pleasers out there.

These lists are a way to validate your feelings and help you make intentional decisions based on tangible facts not emotional feelings about the people you allow into your life. These lists curate an empowering Ideal Community composed of clients, team members, leaders, and personal supporters ready to support you and your goals. Now, let's get to work and define your Attract and Repel Lists!

SUMMARIZE YOUR LISTS

STEP 1: LOOK BACK + CREATE TWO LISTS

Go back and look over your answers from the previous questions and write down the most common words, phrases, behaviors, values, or characteristics you listed describing your most favorite and least favorite people and brands. Take these common characteristics and organize them into two lists.

The first list will be the positive characteristics that you want to attract to your Ideal Community.

The second list will be the negative characteristics that you want to repel from your Ideal Community.

Use the following examples to show how you can take what you wrote and condense it into an Attract or Repel list characteristic:

Example: "I respect people who have high standards, aren't looking to 'half ass' things." I respect people who expect a level of excellence for what they do and who they are with.

Repel Translation: "I want to repel people who look for the quick and easy way. Who aren't ready to do the work."

Attract Translation: "I want to attract people who are driven. I want to attract people who seek excellence.

Example: "I appreciate working with or working for individuals who don't take advantage of me."

Repel Translation: "I want to repel people who don't respect me or value what I do."

Attract Translation: "I want to attract people who respect my time and my talents."

Example: "I love working with clients who are open to trying new things and have a willingness to learn."

Repel Translation: "I want to repel people who are stuck in their ways and not open to learning."

Attract Translation: "I want to attract people who are open minded and curious."

Example: "I like serving people who appreciate working as a team. They enjoy the camaraderie and energy of a group to help new ideas come to life."

Repel Translation: "I want to repel people who don't value or respect other people's opinions."

Attract Translation: "I want to attract people who are community focused and like to work as a team."

Example: "I like being around and serving others who have the same sense of humor as I do. People who don't take life too seriously and are looking for a fun partner as we work together!"

Repel Translation: "I want to repel people with a dull personality and don't respond to my dry humor."

Attract Translation: "I want to attract people who are fun and have a sense of humor."

STEP 2: EXAMPLE LISTS

ATTRACT LIST EXAMPLES

Below are a selection of real life Attract List examples from our Connection Crew. Use them as a source of inspiration and tool to help you even further summarize your Attract List down to 5-10 core characteristics.

Note: Characteristics with an * next to them are the most popular/ most used Attract List characteristics.

ATTRACT INDIVIDUALS:

Who appreciate a DIRECT APPROACH

Who appreciate a SIMPLE APPROACH

Who appreciate a QUIET APPROACH

Who appreciate a KIND APPROACH

Who have a SENSE OF HUMOR

Who have a COMPASSIONATE HEART

Who have GOOD ENERGY*

Who are ACCESSIBLE + READY TO GET THINGS DONE

Who are ACTION TAKERS

Who are APPRECIATIVE*

Who are COLLABORATIVE/A TEAM PLAYER

Who are CURIOUS/TAKE INITIATIVE

Who are DECISIVE/KNOW WHAT THEY WANT

Who are DRIVEN/GROWTH-MINDED

Who are DETAIL-ORIENTED

Who are BIG PICTURE THINKERS

Who are PLANNERS

Who are ENCOURAGING

Who are ENTHUSIASTIC ABOUT THE PROCESS!

Who are FOCUSED ON THE LONG TERM/LONG TERM SOLUTIONS

Who are HONEST + VALUE INTEGRITY*

Who are KIND

Who are LOOKING FOR A LEADER

Who are LOOKING FOR A LUXURY EXPERIENCE + PROPERTY

Who are LOOKING FOR AN ADVISOR/LISTENS TO DIRECTION*

Who are LOOKING FOR AN EDUCATOR/TO LEARN

Who are LOOKING FOR A PARTNER TO HELP THEM FIND SOLUTIONS

Who are LOOKING FOR CONNECTION

Who are LOOKING FOR INSPIRATION/TO BE INSPIRED

Who are LOOKING TO BUILD A RELATIONSHIP*

Who are LOYAL

Who are OPEN COMMUNICATORS

Who are OPEN-MINDED*

Who are POSITIVE*

Who are READY FOR CHANGE!

Who are READY TO LEARN/CURIOUS

Who are REALISTIC*

Who are RESPECTFUL *

Who are TRUSTING*

Who are LOOKING TO GIVE TRUST*

Who are WILLING TO BUY INTO/INVEST IN YOU

Who are WILLING TO ENGAGE

Who are WILLING TO PUT IN THE WORK

Who are WILLING TO REFER*

Who are WILLING TO SHARE THEIR EXPERIENCE

Who can RECOGNIZE + APPRECIATE YOUR VALUE

Who SEEK CALM AND SIMPLICITY

Who SEEK ENERGY + SPUNK

Who SEEK COMFORT

Who SEEK LEADERSHIP

Who VALUE MY EXPERIENCE*

Who VALUE SOCIAL RESPONSIBILITY

Who VALUE EQUALITY

Who VALUE GIVING BACK

Who VALUE MY WORK

Who VALUE SUPPORTING COMMUNITY

Who THINK OUTSIDE OF THE BOX

Who THINK BIGGER

Who THINK ANALYTICALLY

Who RESPECT LEADERSHIP

Who RESPECT OTHERS

Who RESPECT MY BOUNDARIES*

Who RESPECT MY VOICE

Who RESPECT MY TIME*

REPEL LIST EXAMPLES

Below are a selection of characteristics and qualities from a variety of our Connection Crews' Ideal Community Repel Lists. Use them as a source of inspiration and as a tool to help you even further summarize your 5-10 core characteristics of your Repel List.

Note: Characteristics with an * next to them are the most popular/most used Repel List characteristics.

REPEL INDIVIDUALS:

Who are ARGUMENTATIVE*

Who are ARROGANT

Who are ATTRACTED TO OR USE CHEAP SALES TACTICS

Who are ATTRACTED TO QUICK/SHORT TERM TACTICS

Who are CONDESCENDING

Who are DEMANDING

Who are DISHONEST

Who are DISRESPECTFUL

Who are DULL WITH NO ZEST FOR LIFE

Who are HIGH ENERGY

Who are LOW ENERGY

Who are EGOTISTICAL

Who are ENTITLED

Who are FICKLE

Who are HIGHLY EMOTIONAL

Who are INDECISIVE

Who are LACK DISCIPLINE

Who are LOOKING FOR A "CHEAP" EXPERIENCE

Who are MISOGYNISTIC

Who are MICROMANAGERS

Who are NARCISSISTIC/SELF-FOCUSED

Who are NEGATIVE/COMPLAINER

Who are NOT A TEAM PLAYER

Who are NOT AVAILABLE

Who are NOT COACHABLE OR LOOKING TO LEARN

Who are NOT COLLABORATIVE**

Who are NOT COMMITTED TO GOALS/WISHY WASHY

Who are NOT COMPASSIONATE

Who are NOT ENGAGED

Who are NOT INTEGRITY LED*

Who are NOT LOOKING FOR CONNECTION

Who are NOT LOOKING TO BUILD A RELATIONSHIP*

Who are NOT LOOKING TO LEARN

Who are NOT LOYAL

Who are NOT OPEN-MINDED

Who are NOT REALISTIC

Who are NOT TRUSTING*

Who are NOT WILLING TO REFER*

Who are NOT WILLING TO TAKE DIRECTION*

Who are OVERWHELMING

Who are QUESTION YOUR EXPERIENCE/SOLUTIONS*

Who are SEXIST

Who are SUPERFICIAL/DON'T RESPOND TO "REAL"

Who are UNREALISTIC WITH EXPECTATIONS

Who are UNWILLING TO DO THE WORK

Who are WILLING TO TAKE ADVANTAGE OF OTHERS TO GET AHEAD

Who do not RESPECT MY BOUNDARIES

Who do not RESPECT MY TIME

Who do not SEE ME AS A LEADER

Who do not SEE THE BIGGER PICTURE*

Who do not TAKE RESPONSIBLITY

Who do not VALUE COMMUNITY

Who do not VALUE GIVING BACK

Who do not VALUE MY VOICE OR EFFORTS

Who do not VALUE MY WORK

Who do not VALUE SOCIAL JUSTICE AND RESPONSIBILITY

Who have an UNHEALTHY SKEPTICISM

Who LEAD WITH EXCUSES

STEP 3: CREATE YOUR REPEL LIST

It's time to put together your Repel List.

Look back at your summary notes from Step 1 as well as the provided examples. Use these to help you summarize and compile the 5-10 characteristics of who you most want to *repel* from your Ideal Community.

STEP 4: CREATE YOUR ATTRACT LIST

It's time to put together your Attract List.

Look back at your summary notes from Step 1 as well as the provided examples. Use these to help you summarize and compile the 5-10 characteristics of who you most want to attract to your Ideal Community.

STEP 5: DEFINE YOUR THREE NON-NEGOTABLIES

Each characteristic of your Attract and Repel List have value and must be used to filter your Ideal Community, but it is important to identify your top three non-negotiable characteristics for each list. These non-negotiables are your starting point when evaluating who you are attracting and repelling from your Community.

> " Non-negotiables are your starting point when evaluating who you are attracting and repelling from your Community. "

Look back at your Attract and Repel lists and identify the top three characteristics—non-negotiable characteristics—from each list. These are the three core characteristics you will look for, speak to and focus on attracting. You will also define three non-negotiable characteristics you wish to repel from your Community, that act as instant red flags when you start to feel "off" with someone.

Identifying your non negotiables will be a touchpoint you can quickly refer to when filtering your Community or sharing type of expectations you have for your Community.

Whether it is meeting someone new, taking on a new client, investing in leadership or deciding who you spend time around, these non-negotiables will help you to become more aware of the type of people, energy and support you want in your Community.

Look back at your Attract List and find the top three characteristics that make you feel respected, energized, appreciated, and motivated. Find the top three characteristics you most want to attract.

Secondly, look back at your Repel List and find the top three characteristics that make you feel disrespected, unappreciated, and depleted. Find the top three characteristics you most want to repel.

For example, my own personal Attract List non-negotiable characteristics are individuals who 1) have good energy, 2) who respect my time and 3) who are willing to do the work.

My three Repel List non-negotiable characteristics are individuals 1) who do not respect my time, 2) are not looking to genuinely connect, 3) who are negative.

What are yours?

STEP 6: USE YOUR LISTS

It's time to repel and attract!

After completing Steps 3 and 4, you should now have a solid list of characteristics, personality traits and values of who you want to repel from your Ideal Community and who you want to attract to your Ideal Community.

These characteristics apply to your Ideal Community as a whole. Yes, especially for your Ideal Client, but also for your Ideal Team, Ideal Leadership, and Ideal Support Crew. Make sure before allowing people into your Community in any role, that they pass through the Repel and Attract filters first.

Below is an example of what a completed Attract and Repel List can look like (This one is mine!). Just like your Branding Words, I recommend printing off your Attract and Repel Lists and having them in front of you at all time. Memorize this list so you can instinctually know if someone is an Attract Lister or a Repel Lister instantly!

ATTRACT LIST *Kelsey's* REPEL LIST

NON-NEGOTIABLES

#1 Who HAVE GOOD ENERGY

#2 Who RESPECT MY TIME

#3 Who are WILLING TO DO THE WORK

NON-NEGOTIABLES

#1 Who DO NOT RESPECT MY TIME

#2 Who are NOT LOOKING TO CONNECT

#3 Who are NEGATIVE

ATTRACT	REPEL
Who are HONEST + VALUE INTEGRITY	Who LEAD WITH SALES NOT SERVICE
Who are LOOKING FOR CONNECTION	Who are NOT LOOKING TO CONNECT
Who are LOOKING FOR INSPIRATION	Who are NOT POSITIVE
Who are LOOKING TO BE INSPIRED	Who are NOT LOOKING TO LEARN
Who are LOOKING TO BUILD A RELATIONSHIP	Who are CLOSED-MINDED
Who are LOOKING TO LEARN	Who are SUPERFICIAL
Who are ACCESSIBLE	Who LEAD WITH EXCUSES
Who are READY TO GET THINGS DONE	Who are ARROGANT
Who are ACTION TAKERS	Who DON'T RESPOND TO "REAL"
Who are APPRECIATIVE	Who DON'T SEE THE BIGGER PICTURE
Who VOCALIZE THEIR APPRECIATION	Who DON'T RESPECT MY TIME
Who are DRIVEN + GROWTH-MINDED	Who DON'T HAVE GOOD ENERGY
Who are ENTHUSIASTIC ABOUT THE PROCESS!	Who are LOOKING FOR A CHEAP EXPERIENCE
	Who are NEGATIVE + COMPLAIN
	Who are NOT COMMITTED TO GOALS

DEMOGRAPHIC

With Connection-Based Branding, your first job is to define the characteristics of your Ideal Community as a whole. Your Attract and Repel Lists are your filters and checkpoint to see if an individual would be a positive or negative addition to your Community.

A demographic represents the technical characteristics of who you want to attract such as age, sex, relationship status and location. Getting specific with the nitty gritty details of who this person is (how old they are, where they live, what they like to do for fun) helps you understand and connect with your Ideal Community with intention.

In the end, the most important part of your Ideal Community are your Attract and Repel Lists, but depending on what industry you are in and the type of business and/or career you want to build, knowing the demographics of who you want in your Community can be a powerful tool as well. Some of the following questions will apply to you, and some will not. Do your best and remember that "I don't know" or "not applicable" is always an acceptable answer.

PRIMARY + SECONDARY DEMOGRAPHICS:

One last note before you dive into demographics, is that depending on what you offer, whether it is a business service or product, or how you serve in a leadership role, you may end up having multiple demographic profiles.

Primary Demographic is the individual or group directly receiving the service, product or leadership.

Secondary Demographics is an individual or group who is indirectly involved in the process.

For example, if you are a photographer who works primarily with high school seniors, in most cases the parent will be the paying customer. However, the individual receiving the service is the actual high school senior. This is a classic case of Primary and Secondary Demographics, where the high school student is the Primary and the parent is the Secondary.

If this scenario applies to you, please answer the demographic questions twice. Once for your Primary Demographic and once for your Secondary Demographic.

DEMOGRAPHIC: THE QUESTIONS

Just to recap, a demographic refers to specific descriptors of an individual such as, sex, age, income, education, family, religion, industry, location, etc.

Whether or not you feel like a question is applicable to you, go through them anyway. Allow yourself to brainstorm even deeper with who you specifically enjoy serving. Think about your Attract List. Think about the favorite person you described in the previous questions. Are there consistent or similar demographic characteristics of the person you most enjoy working with, serving or being led by? Use them as the example to base your answers.

Don't be afraid of being specific and exclusive. Being focused with who you most want to serve benefits not only you, but your Ideal Community as a whole.

1. **Do you have a specific sex you prefer to work with, connect with or serve?**

   Men? Women? Trans? Non-Binary? Who energizes you the most?

2. **Do you have a specific age range you prefer to work with, connect with or serve?**

   Does working with kids or teens light your fire? Do millennials speak to your soul? Does working with retirees give you the warm fuzzies? What age range energizes you the most?

3. **Do you most enjoy working with people who are married, single, divorced, co-parents, in a partnership?**

   What is their relationship status? Does it matter to you? Why or why not?

4. **Do you enjoy working with individuals who have kids?**

   If so, what stage of life are they in? What ages are their kids? Parents of babies, toddlers, middle school, high school, college, grown adults? Does it matter to you? Why or why not?

5. **Do you enjoy working with individuals who are at a certain income and/or education level?**

   Keep in mind, narrowing down financial demographics are important, but don't let them limit you. If you have what someone wants, they will find the money and/or get the education they need to get it.

6. **Do you most enjoy working with people from a certain area?**

   Do you want to serve people in your immediate town or state? Do you want to serve people in your country or continent? Do you want to serve your Community worldwide? Where are your people from? Where do they live? Anywhere is an acceptable answer if you are global.

7. **Do you enjoy working with individuals who have industry-specific demographics?**

   Such as, first time home buyers, unpublished authors, high-end wedding planners, beginner photographers, executive level leadership, mommy bloggers, tech industry, agriculture, food and beverage, entertainment, construction, fashion, marketing, communications, etc.

8. **What are the biggest struggles or challenges your Ideal Client is experiencing?**

   Think about why they come to you? What are the common words or phrases they tell you when explaining their situation and needs? Is it that they need education, leadership, organization, systems, support, etc.?

9. **What is the biggest roadblock preventing your Ideal Client from achieving their goals?**

Think about the things they say to you in your initial interaction, why are they stuck and seeking help/solutions for moving forward?

10. **How could you help them and address their pain points, struggles and roadblocks?**

What do you offer that could help them? Besides just your end goal offering (product/service) what personal characteristics do you have that will help encourage and guide them along the process?

11. **What is holding your Ideal Client back or blocking them from achieving those goals?**

Is it fear, lack of education, lack of resources, confidence, leadership, direction ...?

12. **What are the specific things you offer that could help your Ideal Client achieve their dreams and goals?**

Think about your process. Think about your experience. Think about your story. Think about your perspective. What can you uniquely bring them to help them?

DEMOGRAPHIC: CREATE YOUR "I HELP STATEMENT"

Look back at your answers to the demographic questions and use them to fill in the blank and create your "I Help Statement."

I help _____ (gender and/or family status) _____

Who are _____(age range *if applicable*) _____

Who live _____(location *if applicable*) _____

Who struggle with ___(pain points and challenges) _____

I help them _____ (the solution you offer) _____

Use your "I Help Statement" to help you get even more specific with who you attract, market to or team up with in your Ideal Community. Remember, your first step is to always start with your Attract and Repel Lists and then your demographic specifics.

WHAT IF I'M NOT ATTRACTING THE RIGHT PEOPLE?

"What if I define my Ideal Community and I'm not attracting the type of people I really want?"

I'm going to share the answer to this common question with all the Branding Mama Bear love I have in my heart, but it still may sting a little. You ready? The reason you aren't attracting people from your Attract List is because of one thing ... you. If you are attracting your Repel List, chances are you are on your own Repel List.

> **" If you are attracting your Repel List,**
> **chances are you are on your own Repel List. "**

You are the reflection of the energy that comes back to you.

Your actions, your behavior, your energy, your words, your blocks and your mindset are the things that are preventing your Ideal Community from showing up.

You are the one not respecting yourself, which allows others an open invite to not respect you.

You are the one who is not respecting your own time, so your Community doesn't respect your time.

You are the one who is closed-minded and not ready to learn, that's why you are attracting a Community who are not open minded and set in their ways.

You are the one who is getting in the way of receiving the most incredible leadership from coming into your life.

You are the one who is allowing negative friends and family to continue to disrespect you and take advantage of you.

Bottom line, you attract energy that you put out into the world. If that energy is negative, you'll receive negative. If you are angry, you'll receive anger. If you don't value yourself, others won't value you. If you are scattered, you'll receive scattered.

The opposite is true as well.

If you are loving (not people pleasing), you will receive love. If you are truthful, you will receive truth. If you are hopeful, you will receive hope. If you are respectful, you will receive respect. If you are inspiring, you will receive inspiration. If you are seeking solutions, the solutions will find you. If you are committed, then individuals who are looking to commit will find you.

Get the picture?

This energy exchange is not some spiritual woo-woo mystical banter. It's science. It's physics. It's the Law of Attraction, which is based on Sir. Isaac Newton's Third Law of Motion. Simply put, Newton's Third Law is: for every action there is an equal and opposite reaction. Everything you do (physically, emotionally, financially, spiritually, etc.) is coming back to you every second of the day.

You hold the power of flipping the switch and changing your perspective from negative to positive, victim to victor, from disempowered to empowered, insecure to secure, fearful to hopeful and from scarcity to grateful.

Your Ideal Community Attract List is here for you to help attract the correct energy you wish to welcome into your Community. The key is that you must be the example and show up as your own Attract List. Your Ideal Community is waiting for you. It's your job to fiercely respect and protect your Attract Listers them against the Repel Listers. Grab your can of repellent "Psst-Psst."

IDEAL COMMUNITY
Wrap Up

As we wrap up this chapter, I want to leave you with the spirit of hope and tangible direction for where to focus your limited, and oh, so precious time, energy, and resources.

I want you to confidently know that you hold the key to having the Ideal Community you truly desire. A kickass Community composed of the Clients, Team Members, Leadership, and Support Crew of your dreams. Focus on attracting your Ideal Community by letting your personal energy reflect your Attract List, and don't settle for people or opportunities that reflect your Repel List.

Focus on attracting your Ideal Community by letting your personal energy reflect your Attract List, and don't settle for people or opportunities that reflect your Repel List.

Refer to your Attract and Repel Lists on the daily. Integrate your Attract List characteristics into your daily narrative in conversations, on your website and on social media. Make it easy for people to know exactly who you serve so the path of attracting the right people is simple.

Once you do that, watch how the Law of Attraction kicks in by giving back to you the positive energy, people and opportunities that have been waiting for you.

Chapter Recap

IDEAL COMMUNITY

In this chapter you learned:

⇨ **The difference between an Ideal Client and Ideal Community**

⇨ **What an Ideal Community is, and the importance of defining a broader vision for who you attract.**

- The four groups within an Ideal Community

- Ideal Client

- Ideal Team

- Ideal Leadership

- Ideal Support Crew

⇨ **How to define your Ideal Community**

⇨ **How to define your Attract List**

⇨ **How to define your Repel List**

⇨ **The Law of Attraction**

CHAPTER SEVEN

THE GAP

"What makes you different or weird, that's your strength."

- MERYL STREEP, ACTRESS

One of my favorite places to sneak away for a quick weekend getaway is to my friend Rae's cozy mountain cabin. It's a rustic, tiny cabin nestled on a river in Washington's beautiful Cascade Mountain Range.

On one of my cabin visits, Rae and I were cozied up on her couch, when out of the blue, she said, "I've thought about writing a book. A book that shares my passion for women in the tech world, but also about how to add rest to their lives while working in the high-paced tech industry."

As she told me more, I saw the passion for this topic sparkle in her eyes. The energy in her voice was intoxicating. Even though I knew nothing about the tech world and computer coding (Rae's specialty), I was sold!

But then, as if a giant brick wall landed in the middle of her passion-filled path, she stopped and said, "But Kels, who would even read it? Why should I put myself out there if there are so many other people who already do what I do and teach what I teach?"

The sudden halt of her inspiration flabbergasted me. Her idea entranced me. I wanted more. There was no way I would let her get away with that kind of questioning-her-greatness thinking! So, I took off my proverbial hoop earrings and heels, got up on my soapbox, and prepared to dish some truth.

I told her, "Rae Rae! What are you talking about?! Sure, your industry is massive and filled with a ton of smart, techy people, but none of them are you! You are unique. Your story and experiences are unique. You have your own unique message. You provide your own unique value. You have something different to offer because it is from YOU! Your industry may be saturated, but it isn't saturated with Raes, because there is only one YOU—so leverage that!"

As I took a breath, she nodded in agreement, and then I kept going.

I said, "Rae, all you have to do is define what makes you different, and share that! Use what makes you different to connect, inspire others, and impact your industry. What makes you different is your secret weapon. Even if your industry is inundated with voices, your voice is one of a kind. Your voice has value and is so needed!"

This impassioned speech is not only how I feel about Rae's situation, but it is also how I feel about you, too.

The lesson to take from this is that no matter how saturated your industry seems to be, there *is a place for you.*

Consider my profession; I am a photographer.

It seems like *everybody* and their mother calls themselves a photographer these days! But guess what? My work and my voice still have value. So does yours.

The key to navigating this saturation and finding your own place is to find what makes you different, or as I call it, The Gap.

> " The key to navigating this saturation and finding your own place is to find what makes you different, or as I call it, The Gap. "

Finding your Gap is about finding that untouched space that only *you* can fill with your experience, your talents, your passions, your voice, and your unique perspective. It's about exploring, defining, and owning what specifically makes you different so you can establish your own place and fill the Gap meant for you.

The best way to understand The Gap concept is to take a trip to imagination land with me. Imagine taking everyone in your industry and lining them up shoulder to shoulder in a single-file line. They are lined up, facing you, and looking straight at you. This line is vast, seemingly never ending, and is ridiculously intimidating.

The intimidation factor is real because this line not only has a lot of people in it, but is made up of people with incredible talent, diverse ideas, and professional skills. People who have experience, education and creative ideas that seem so out of reach.

As you look at this line, it probably feels so overwhelming that fear, self-doubt, and the Comparison Monster show up. This Monster whispers doubt and insecurity in your ear, questioning your worthiness so you stand there, paralyzed.

As you stare wide-eyed at this huge lineup of high-quality, mind-blowing people in front of you, you take a moment, and look down. And when you do, you see that you have a backpack sitting at your feet.

Out of curiosity, you crouch down and unzip the top of the bag to peek inside. Inside you see this bag is filled with elements of you. Is filled with your story, and the things that make you different. It's packed with the things that make you, you. This backpack is full of your Sasquatch Factor. Remember that from the beginning of the book?

Your Sasquatch Factor. The things that make you unique, different, and stand out. Your education. Your personal and professional experiences. Your unique perspective. Your sense of humor. Your hobbies. Your childhood experiences. Your adventures throughout life. Your natural talents. Your worldview. The lessons you've learned along the way. All the things that set you apart are your Sasquatch Factor and are contained in this backpack sitting at your feet.

This backpack is yours. It holds what is uniquely you. Some contents are joyful, some are confusing or painful, but all of them together make you who you are.

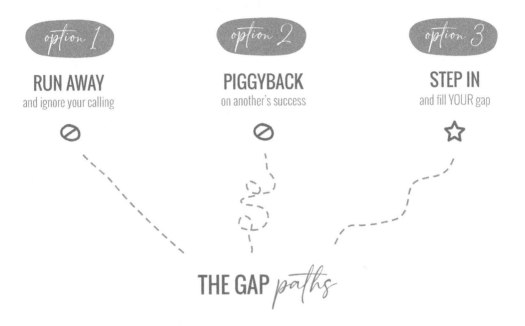

After taking in the contents of your backpack, you decide to zip up your bag and throw the straps over your shoulders and look up at the line in front of you.

It's at this moment, your heart races, and you realize you have three options.

The first option is that you look at the line and say, "No way! That line is too long! There is no space for me!"

Out of fear, impatience, frustration, and insecurity, you decide to drop your backpack on the ground, turn your back to the line and run the other way. You decide to not join the line at all. Fear gets the best of you, so you ignore your calling and, in turn, ignore the people who so desperately need to hear your voice.

The second option is to get uncomfortably intimate with someone else already in line and claim *their* space as your own.

With this option, you discard your backpack, and you step into someone else's Gap. You hop onto them, piggybacking like a baby koala and take on their vision and voice as your own.

You figure, the line has already accepted them, they are successful, it's safe to copy them, so it should guarantee success for me, too.

However, that's not how it works. After a while, piggybacking on someone else gets tiring. It's uncomfortable (and your leg is probably starting to cramp). It's not feeling right because you are contorting yourself into a space that was not meant for you. Besides, piggybacks are for children, not for leaders.

The third option (which, spoiler alert! is the one I recommend you go with) is where you cinch down the straps of your backpack, approach the line, and step into a gap in the line. This Gap is *your* Gap.

This Gap has your name on it and has been waiting for you. It's been open and ready for you to claim it, so now's the time. By stepping into your Gap, you are owning a space which is rightfully yours.

When you step into your Gap, you now have a place where you can unpack your backpack, own what makes you different, plant your feet and proudly proclaim, "This is me!"

This Gap is all yours. It's a place for you to grow, stretch, evolve and most importantly, connect with others and impact them with your unique story and your unique voice. By stepping into your Gap, you have decided to own what makes you different. You've decided to own who you are.

In doing so, you have opened the door for others to connect, feel seen, heard and know that they matter by telling your story with your Connection-Based Brand.

At first, it may feel lonely and you question if you are doing it right, but as others start feeling connected to your voice and feel seen through your offering, you will feel more confident in your unique space, and eventually, your industry will take notice. It just takes time, grit, and patience.

DON'T GO THE SELFISH ROUTE

If you go with option one or two, and not to step into your unique Gap in line, this decision is an incredibly selfish act. Yes, selfish.

When you decide that your voice and message aren't worth sharing, you are indirectly telling the people who are seeking to connect with you that *they don't matter*. When you say no to your Gap, you are also simultaneously saying no to serving others who need you.

Sharing what makes you different and stepping into your Gap is a selfless act.

I have had some clients come to me and think that the opposite is true. That they come off as selfish or self-focused if they share what makes them different and share their story. But that is not the case. Sharing what makes you different and stepping into your Gap is a selfless act.

There is a group of people out there, your Community, who feel alone, who don't feel seen, or feel like they matter. It doesn't matter if the line is saturated with people, this group of people, your Community, is waiting to connect with you. They are primed to give trust and are yearning to connect with *you—not someone else.*

BEAUTY INDUSTRY: DISRUPTED

One of my favorite examples of a business owner finding, and owning their unique Gap is R&B artist, Robyn "Rihanna" Fenty and her cosmetics line, Fenty Beauty.

With the entire beauty industry valued at over $500 billion dollars, the beauty industry is the definition of an oversaturated market. It seemed like there was no space left for something new. It seemed like everyone was packed in so tightly that there were no Gaps left. That is, until Fenty Beauty came along.

In 2017, Rihanna launched her Fenty Beauty brand with one mission: to focus on promoting and celebrating diversity. Fenty Beauty launched a revolutionary makeup line that had never been done before, one that included foundation colors for *every* skin color. Before Fenty Beauty, people of color struggled to find the right makeup to match to their skin tone. There had always been plentiful options in ivories, beiges, and tans, but darker skin tones were left with limited options. Fenty Beauty changed that.

In addition to offering an expanded color makeup line, Fenty Beauty also celebrated diversity by using real men, women, and non-binary individuals in their marketing campaigns who represented different ethnicities, sizes, and skin tones, and sourced directly from their Fenty Beauty community. Even though the beauty industry was overly saturated, Fenty Beauty saw their Gap, stepped into it and claimed it as their own.

Because Fenty Beauty didn't let the fear of an oversaturated industry stop them from stepping into and owning their "place in-line," a diverse group of makeup lovers are finally feeling seen, recognized, and valued by an industry that had overlooked them for years.

Because their customers felt seen and connected with the values and mission of the brand, they reciprocated this connection with their dollars. In the first 15 months of business, Fenty Beauty did $570 million business and is now, in 2021, worth an estimated $3 billion dollars. Yep. Epic mic drop.

The beauty industry couldn't ignore this success. As a result, other beauty brands started following in Fenty's footsteps by including a broader spectrum of foundation colors and incorporated diversity and inclusivity in their marketing.

Fenty Beauty stands as a prime example of the domino effect of impact when you step into your Gap and own what makes you different. When you stay true to you and confidently own your Gap in line, in time, everyone else in line will take notice and recognize the impact you're creating. This impact is then able to gain momentum and ripple out to inspire change and growth in your industry overall. That's the power of owning your Gap.

PERSONAL PAIN IS THE GREATEST CONNECTION TOOL

Defining your Gap is not only what makes you different in the professional world, but also what makes you different in your personal life and story. Your personal story is where the deepest levels of connection can formulate and grow.

I learned about the power of defining your personal Gap and the importance of sharing your story early on in life. I was raised in an angry home, where fear and rage were the currency and where you felt more like an inconvenience rather than a joy. My father was the main source of anger. He used anger driven actions and words which caused years of fear for my sister, mother, and me.

When I was around 8 or 9, my mother tucked me in one night and said, "I know our family struggles, but don't let it define you. You are going through this for a reason, a bigger reason. One day, you will hear that someone else is going through the same thing you did, and your story can be an encouragement for them, so they won't feel alone. That's the reason we go through hard things, it's so we can help others by sharing our story."

I took my mother's advice to heart and have intentionally lived it out both the personal and professional areas of my life. In my experience, you never really know what's going on behind closed doors, so if you use your story as a tool for service and a tool for connection, then impact, inspiration, and empowering others is able to thrive.

> " Your personal story is where the deepest levels of connection can formulate and grow. "

Define and share your Connection-Based Brand through the lens of what makes you different, both personally and professionally. Once you do, your Community can say, "Me too. I see myself in your story. I'm not alone after all. I connect to you and trust you."

That's what this chapter is about, looking at your story from a perspective of service to help and connect with others. To help you become a Connection-Based Leader who has a Connection-Based Brand rooted in your real and unique history. Your story is the secret to defining what makes you different.

IMPOSTER SYNDROME

In a perfect world full of gumdrops, rainbows, and kitten kisses, stepping into your Gap will magically bestow upon you unwavering confidence where you're unbothered with insecurity and self-doubt. I am here to tell you, that's not going to happen.

Nope. The truth is, owning your Gap is incredibly empowering but also an incredibly scary and a vulnerable place to be. Chances are, if you haven't met The Imposter Syndrome along the way, you will while defining your Gap.

The Imposter Syndrome tends to sink in when you are about to take another step towards your goals. You are stepping out of your comfort zone, challenging your current status quo, and following the prompts of your greater purpose. It's exciting, but also scary and prime pickin's for the Imposter Syndrome to cause havoc.

Our brain has rationalized that the only way to compensate for big moves is to allow the Imposter Syndrome to come in and join the party. It plops themself onto your confidence couch and tells you things like:

"Who do you think you are?"

"You're not experienced enough or smart enough to do this!"

"Everybody else is doing this. They have more experience, skills and knowledge, you're a joke and wasting everyone's time!"

"Who are you to lead these people? There are much more qualified people than you."

We've all been there, am I right? When this feeling hits, I remember something one of my best friends once told me, "From everything I've seen about Imposter Syndrome, it's usually experienced by people who aren't imposters. But rather by people who know what it means to do great work and provide great value, and they're being given a new opportunity that is going to stretch their capabilities beyond what they've been doing. So, they aren't an imposter, they're just leveling up."

That's it. Defining your Connection-Based Brand and stepping into your Gap is you leveling up to your greater purpose. Others are waiting for you, so it's time to level up and tell the Imposter Syndrome they aren't welcome here anymore.

BENEFITS OF DEFINING YOUR GAP

Sharing what makes you different, your Gap, is the most impactful action you can take for yourself, your Brand, and your Community. Owning your Gap gives you permission to be yourself, defines tangible connection pieces, and shifts your focus from your competition to those you serve.

Being yourself and owing your Gap is the greatest way to serve others. When you own your Gap, only good can come out of it. By defining and owning your Gap, it can benefit you in three specific ways:

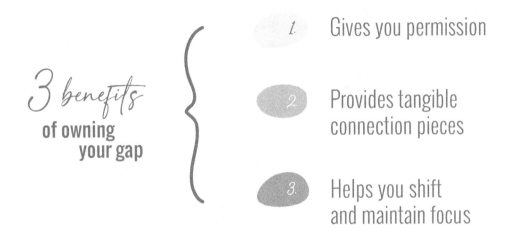

3 benefits
**of owning
your gap**

1. Gives you permission

2. Provides tangible connection pieces

3. Helps you shift and maintain focus

BENEFIT 1: GIVES YOU PERMISSION

Defining your Gap not only helps you find yourself, but it also gives you permission to be yourself. It keeps you in check when you start to drift and try to conform or piggyback onto someone else's identity. Defining and owning your Gap is a literal permission slip to be yourself.

Before *The Connection Method*, my client Louise said she was in a constant cycle of second guessing herself, downplaying her bold personality and creative spirit. She would change her identity, adjust her personality to match the person she was talking to, and would even alter what she wore in order to fit into assumed expectations.

> " Defining and owning your Gap is a literal permission slip to be yourself. "

After completing *The Connection Method* and defining her Gap, Louise realized that what made her different and living out her true self was what her Community actually wanted to see and experience! She told me that she's proud of who she is and can now go into client meetings or new opportunities, confident that she is more than enough just as herself.

She told me, before defining her Connection-Based Brand:

"I would question whether I should wear a hot pink blazer and show my big and vivacious personality. Now, I wear that hot pink blazer with pride and confidence! In fact, people now have come to expect my bold style and personality. I have defined what my clients and Community can expect, so when I show up as me, they don't question it. They feel more confident in my consistency. And, if I feel like I need to change who I am for a potential client or opportunity, I know instantly that it's not an opportunity I want to take on or a person I would want to work with!"

BENEFIT 2: PROVIDES TANGABLE CONNECTION PIECES

Defining your Gap provides tangible connection pieces. These connection pieces move away from just feeling something about a person or brand, but tangibly identifying the actual things that connect us.

Whether they are the stories, the values, the personality, or struggles of a certain person or brand, these are the pieces that genuinely connect us. Whether it is the deepest of struggles like poverty, eating disorders, depression, or abuse, or simple fun facts like growing up in the same town, loving the same TV show, sharing a passion for comic book heroes, or sharing the same type of humor, identifying, and sharing pieces of your story are the first elements that connect us to each other. These connection pieces—even the most insignificant ones—lay the foundation for building trust with others.

My client, Elizabeth, lives in Washington State, but is originally from Long Island, New York. A Long Island woman through and through, her passion for her home town echoed throughout her heart, personality and even her approach to business.

When she had a meeting with a new client, she found out that this woman was not only from Long Island as well, but also the same neighborhood Elizabeth was from!

When they each learned this, these two Long Island ladies instantly felt connected. Just from the one, simple connection piece of their hometown, it was as if the magical fingers of connection snapped and they instantly felt a deep level of connection and trust between them.

For the rest of the afternoon, they excitedly shared stories, memories, and their favorite spots back home. They didn't talk business, they talked story. These stories were the tangible connection pieces which deepened their trust, respect, and emotional connection to each other. Just because they were from the same town, it laid the foundation for personal and eventually, a professional connection.

When you find and share what makes you different (your Gap), your unique story creates provides a powerful path of impact. By sharing your Gap with your Community, you become a vessel of connection, so others feel like their story and voice have value too.

BENEFIT 3: HELPS YOU SHIFT AND MAINTAIN FOCUS

The third core benefit of defining your Gap is that it helps shift your focus from everyone in the industry lineup to focusing on who really matters, your Community. It helps you to focus on your Community, not your competition.

Your Gap stands as a reminder that your place in line is intentional, not accidental. Your Gap has purpose and provides your unique value to your Community. It stands as a reminder of who you are, so you don't get swayed or distracted by what everyone else in line is doing.

When the Imposter Syndrome creeps in or the Comparison Monster whispers doubt in your ear, our knee jerk response is to look at what others are doing in our industry and compare ourselves. We question if we are good enough, or if we are doing it "right," because our story is different, we look different, lead differently, speak differently, or approach business differently than others in our industry.

Instead of looking to your competition to determine if you are doing it right, let your Community be your sounding board. Shift your focus and energy to serving your Community with your unique offering. Shift your focus and energy to the people who are waiting for and yearning for what you have to offer, not your competition.

> ## Focus on your Community, not your competition.

One of my clients, Ingrid, is a luxury realtor but prides herself on not being your typical luxury broker. She is approachable, down-to-earth and has a fun and snappy personality. However, when she attends luxury broker meetings and events, she always feels less than and finds herself trying to fit into everyone else's story. She always tried to fit into their Gap, not her own.

She would intentionally go out of her way to buy and wear designer clothes to these events. She would feel embarrassed when her one-million-dollar listing would pop up on display at the meetings, since the ones before and after hers were $20+ million-dollar homes. She was so focused on being enough for her peers, that she completely forgot and ignored the fact that she needed to be enough for her own Community.

When she shared this story with me, I told her the only way to overcome this was to shift her focus from her competition to her Community. I remind her that there is a group of people literally waiting for her to step into her Gap and show up as herself.

I told her to imagine the giant line up of people in your industry are standing to your left, and then on your right, is your Ideal Community. The people standing to your right are your people. Your Crew. Your Attract Listers. They are eagerly waiting to work with you. They desire to value you, support you and share your brand with the world!

However, if you're telescoping your focus and attention solely on the left group, on your competition, it means you are ignoring your Community. You are ignoring the people who are waiting for you to own your Gap. You are ignoring the people who want you to unzip your backpack, pull out all the amazing things that make you unique and tell them all about your Sasquatch Factor. They are waiting for you to shift your focus to them, so don't ignore the people who matter and who need you.

They are looking for you.

They are waiting for you.

They are ready for you.

So, give them your attention.

Show up and serve them.

Focus on your Community, not your competition.

DEFINE YOUR GAP: THE QUESTIONS

The first part of this chapter was my not-so-subtle attempt to tell you that you are enough.

You are enough. Right now, just as you are.

Who you are, your story, your hurts, your joys, your failures and your successes are enough. Your story, your personality, your approach, the things that make you different are the things that people need to see!

You might not think your story and who you are is anything special, but it is. Who you are is something special to others, and could help others who are seeking the kind of connection your story provides. By owning your Gap, you allow others to connect with you and know that they matter in this world. You help others feel that they are not alone. That's the power of your so-called, "not anything special" story can provide. Because it is special and it is powerful.

It's always hard to define how you are different. We see our experiences and our world as ordinary and nothing exceptional. But you are exceptional, and so is your story.

In order to help you define your Gap, I've provided a list of questions to help tangibly define what makes you different. To help you define something your Community can connect with.

As you go through the questions, please remember a few basic rules that you agreed to at the beginning of *The Connection Method*.

First, that you won't overthink your answers. There are no right or wrong answers. Go with your gut.

Secondly, don't strive for perfect answers. The messier they are, the better. Be honest with yourself, even if it hurts or is embarrassing. Dig deep, because the deeper you go, the more genuine and real you can be with yourself and others!

Thirdly, don't be afraid to speak highly of yourself. Even if you feel like you are bragging. You have incredible and unique experiences and talents to offer, be sure to share them in your answers and don't downplay them!

Trigger Warning: Everyone's story is different, and we all have experienced different hurt, pain, and trauma. Some of these questions might open old wounds or experiences. Please take the following questions at your own pace and with care.

QUESTION SET 1 OF 2: PERSONAL

1. **On a daily basis, how often do you feel like you show up as your true self?**
   Are you yourself all-day-everyday, right in the middle, or are you not living as your true self?

2. **What are you most proud of about yourself?**
   Please let go of any fear of coming off as self-involved. This is the time to tell yourself how proud you are of who you are as a person and as a professional. I give you full permission to speak highly of yourself!

3. **What are you most proud of from your personal life story?**
   Think about life circumstances that you have overcome, but most importantly don't just think about the end result. Don't just say "having kids" or "getting the career of your dreams." Instead, think about the process of getting there and what it's been like to maintain it.

4. **What has made you a strong and determined human?**

   I know you may not feel like it, but you are so incredibly strong! You have made it through so much! What do you think helped you get this far?

5. **Growing up, what were the biggest struggles or challenges you and/or your family went through?**

   Think about your family's story, did you experience poverty, immigrant family/personal immigration, bullies, incarceration, divorce, abuse, lack of self-confidence, trouble in school, etc.

6. **Given your history, are you surprised with where you are at now?**

   Why or why not?

7. **What is something people would be surprised to learn about you?**

   Think about hidden talents or the different experiences you've had in your life. Think about your go-to answer when someone asks for a fun fact about you.

8. **What makes you "weird?"**

   We all have something a little strange about us, our story or how we did business. What are your own "weird" factors?

9. **What makes you "boring?"**

   Connection can also be found in the most simple, mundane, and "boring" things. Do you love a certain type of coffee? Do you eat the same meal every day? Do you wear the same outfit to work? How do you conduct work? How do you run your family? Think about the most seemingly insignificant factors of your life because they matter too!

10. **What does a typical day look like for you?**

    Connection can be found in the ordinary. Describe your typical day at work from when you wake up to when you shut down the computer. What tools do you use to do your work? What planning is involved? Tell me the story of your typical day! Side note: be sure to show this answer to your photographer when you do a Lifestyle Branding Photoshoot (more on this in a later chapter)!

11. **What do you like to do outside of work?**

    Tell me about the activities that are life-giving to you! Is it hiking, biking, swimming, figure skating, rock climbing, cookie decorating, knitting, reading, wine tasting, traveling? Be as specific as you can, since these are often the first connection pieces others will feel a connection with you. These activities are door-openers for you to connect. Also, show this answer to your Lifestyle Branding Photographer!

12. **What does a perfect day look like to you?**

Tell me about your perfect day. What do you do? Where do you go? Who are you with? What do you eat? What do you wear? Give me all the juicy details!

13. What is the biggest thing you are confident about yourself?

Again, allow yourself to brag about how great you are! What are you most confident about?

14. What is something you could talk about for hours and never get bored?

This can be work related or personal related, what topic(s) light your fire?

15. What are your guilty pleasures?

Reality TV, binging shows, chocolate, junk food, creeping on social media, playing stupid games on your phone, always buying a certain item, singing in the car etc.

16. What do you value above everything else?

I know we have deeply explored your values in the previous chapters, but this is a good time to revisit them and write them down again in a quick and summarized form.

17. What was the most fearful moment or time in your life?

What happened and how did you overcome it?

18. What is your biggest insecurity?

Not enough education? Body image? Your face or skin? Constantly overthinking? Imposter Syndrome? Comparison Monster? Judgement? No one cares about you? You feel alone? If people saw the "real" you, they wouldn't like you?

19. If you knew you couldn't fail, what would you do?

Throw fear out the window, you have a clear pass to success, what would you do? Personally? Professionally?

20. What is your biggest motivating factor behind why you do what you do?

What is your pilot light? Why are you doing this? Why are you in this business or career? Why are you in this personal relationship? Why do you live where you live? There is no right or wrong answer to this, it doesn't even have to be a grand reason. Why do you do what you do?

QUESTION SET 2 OF 2: PROFESSIONAL

Before we move on, can I just tell you that I am so proud of you! No, really, like super-duper proud! It's like you just won an Academy Award, and I am the loudest one clapping and woot-wooting you from the front row of the audience! So. Damn. Proud!

You just worked through and answered some incredibly difficult questions. Maybe you only read through them and haven't answered yet, or you were only able to answer a few, or maybe you worked through each and every one of them. No matter where you are at, the fact you are now processing these questions to define what makes you different is no small feat.

The answers you provide define the most impactful pieces of your personal story, allowing you to connect with people on the deepest levels.

Now, let's dive into the second and final set of questions for The Gap. These questions focus on your professional story and your relationship to your business, career, and industry.

Do the best you can and remember the rules we discussed above. Don't over think it, and don't strive for perfect, because the messiest answers are the best answers. Even if you don't have a clear answer, keep going.

1. **How are you similar to those in your industry?**
   Think about the characteristics that you share with your favorite (or maybe your least favorite) people or leaders in your industry. Think about your competitors, colleagues, and leadership etc. What traits do you share? How are you similar?

2. **How are you different from those in your industry?**
   Now think about those same people and what is the biggest difference between you and them? Are you piggybacking onto someone else's identity, so there aren't any differences, or have you realized that you offer certain unique things?

3. **What is the status quo of your industry?**
   What are the things that "have always been?" What are the current belief systems, values or practices that are the "norm?"

Think about industry brand narratives, the values of people
and businesses in your industry, accepted behaviors, actions or
practices. Tell me the good and the bad.

4. **What are the biggest holes in your industry?**

   Where is your industry lacking in service, coverage, or product?
   Feel free to look around at comparable entrepreneurs, businesses
   and/or leaders. What is their brand narrative saying/not saying?
   What is not being offered?

5. **What do you offer that fills those holes in your industry?**
   How could you shift the status quo?

   Where do you fit in? Where do you stand out? What can you do to
   fill the holes in your industry? What can you do to shift the status
   quo? What could your voice bring to the table?

6. **How would you describe your approach to business or**
   role as a leader?

   Feel free to use your Branding Words! What perspective do you
   have when stepping into a basic day at work or when you are
   launching into a big project or up leveling your career?

7. **If you have been in business/leadership for more than 5**
   years, why would you say your long-term clients, team
   members, or employers are still with you?

   Tell me the biggest factor for why they are sticking around? Think
   back to appreciative conversations or correspondence. What do

they say?

8. **If you have been in business/leadership for less than 5 years, what would you say your current clients, team members or employees appreciate most about you/what you offer?**

Tell me the biggest factor for why your current/recent clients are hiring you and/or referring you? Think back to appreciative conversations or correspondence. What do they say?

DEFINE YOUR GAP

Just like how you defined the characteristics of your Ideal Community, you will be defining your Gap characteristics. You will be taking the answers from the previous questions and summarizing your Gap into 5-10 characteristics in each category:

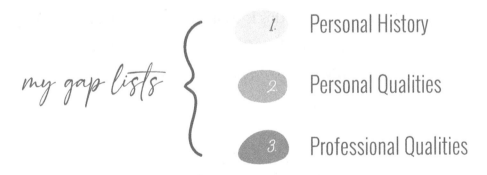

my gap lists

1. Personal History

2. Personal Qualities

3. Professional Qualities

STEP 1: LOOK FOR REPETETION

Look back at your answers and notes from the previous questions and look for any similar and repetitive words and phrases.

Identify the biggest pieces of your story that made you "feel" something. Whether it is pride, excitement, joy or sadness, anger or hurt, those answers are going to be some of your key connection pieces that define your Gap characteristics.

If you notice similarities between characteristics, traits, values, or behaviors, feel free to summarize or combine them into one trait. For example, if you said, "I am driven," "I am focused," and "I am motivated", combine it into one characteristic on your list as "I am driven, focused and motivated." This process is about summarizing your unique traits so you can easily refer to them when connecting with others in person or online.

After writing down repetitive words and phrases from your answers, look through the following examples for inspiration to help you summarize your Gap characteristics and elements even further. Identify any characteristics that you connect with or summarize what you said in your answers. These examples are just suggestions, you can always deviate from this list. After all, this is your story, and your story is unique.

Trigger Warning: *Just like with the preceding questions, there are some sensitive (possible trigger) topics listed in the examples, so read with care.*

GAP EXAMPLES

PERSONAL HISTORY

You have a big personality

You are an extrovert

You have a quiet personality

You are an introvert

You are an omnivert (50% extrovert/50% introvert)

You are a victor not a victim

Your home country

Your hometown

Your family history + upbringing

You grew from your pain

You come from an immigrant family

You come from a military family

You come from a divorced family

You come from a religious family

You have been through a divorce

You have been married for a long time

You are a newlywed

You have experienced a healthy relationship

You have experienced an abusive relationship

You have overcome _____

You have experienced racial injustice

You have experienced sexism

You have experienced prejudice

You have experienced ridicule + judgment for being your true self

You have experienced homelessness

You have experienced poverty

You have experienced financial hardship

You have experienced wealth

You have experienced immigration

You have failed in school

You have struggled in school

You have excelled in school

You have struggled with anxiety

You have struggled with body image

You have struggled with depression

You love an active lifestyle

You love bold colors

You love neutral colors

You love cats

You love dogs

You love food and drink
(get specific)

You love the outdoors

You love to travel

You love to entertain friends
and family

You love to entertain people with
your personality and talents

PERSONAL QUALITIES

You are young

You are middle aged

You are older

You are a leader

You are a supporter

You are an encourager

You are a gifted teacher

You are a gifted speaker

You are an effective negotiator

You are approachable

You are inaccessible

You are a resource

You are classy

You are a rebel

You are funny

You are dependable and reliable

You are a grandparent

You are a parent

You are a step-parent

You are adopted or a foster parent

You are an aunt

You are an uncle

You don't have children

You struggle with infertility

You are a dad with a
high-level career

You are a mom with a
high-level career

You are a single person with a
high-level career

You are a part of the
LGBTQ+ community

You are a supporter of the
LGBTQ+ community

You are passionate about
equal rights

You are passionate about civil rights

You are passionate about
social justice

You enjoy sharing your story

You are real

You have a big picture vision

You have a caring spirit

You have a deep faith

You have an eye for design
and aesthetics

You have a tenacious spirit

You have confidence

You have a competitive spirt

You have insecurities

You have compassion and empathy

You value and lead with integrity

You value others and their story

You value transparency

PROFESSIONAL QUALITIES

You are young.

You have a fresh perspective
on your industry and ready
for experience.

You are middle aged.

You are older.

You have experience stepping into
leadership, but still have a desire
to learn and grow.

You have experience and wisdom.

You are driven

You are focused

You are motivated

You are relationship first focused
vs transaction first focused

You are unafraid of
productive confrontation

You have a stealth approach
to confrontation

You have a goal to be 100% referral based

You have a long-term approach

You have a clear vision for your future

You have a competitive spirit

You have a passion for community involvement

You have a passion for what you do

You have a solutions-based strategy

You have a system-based strategy

You have seasoned industry knowledge

You have special certifications or degrees

You have years of experience

You have just started

You focus on luxury clients and offerings

You focus on mid-level clients and offerings

You focus on entry level clients and offering

STEP 2: SUMMARIZE

Once you have gone through the examples and compiled all your answers, summarize them into 5-10 core Gap characteristics per category.

PERSONAL HISTORY

Summarize your top 5-10 Gap characteristics of your personal history. Think about your unique story, your perseverance, and what helped you get here.

PERSONAL QUALITIES

Summarize your top 5-10 Gap characteristics of your personal qualities. Think about your personality, behavior and values, even if it is the simplest thing, what makes you different?

PROFESSIONAL QUALITIES

Summarize your top 5-10 Gap characteristics of your professional qualities. Think about your Branding Words, what people can expect from you, special perspectives, talents, or education you bring to the table.

EXAMPLE: KELSEY'S GAP CHARACTERISTICS

On the next page is a table featuring my Gap characteristics. It is so important to see how these characteristics can be summarized in a real and tangible way. I hope my Gap can inspire you!

Use this list of personal and professional Gap characteristics to share who you are with your Ideal Community. Use them to tell your story on your "about me" page on your website, to genuinely connect with others in personal conversations, on social media, in marketing campaigns, or on a job interview. Use them to help others in a painful situation, and to remind them that they can get through it because you did as well.

Steve Jobs once said, "You can't connect the dots looking forward, you can only connect them looking backwards," and that's what I hope you can do. Look back at your story, look back and where you came from. That way, you're able to move forward and use it in partnership with

Kelsey's GAP CHARACTERISTICS

PERSONAL HISTORY

I have a big personality

I am an omnivert

I grew up in Mammoth Lakes, California

I grew up in Bellingham, Washington

I enjoy quality time with friends

I have been through a divorce

I have experienced homelessness

I struggled in school

I struggle with dyslexia

I grew up with an angry father

I struggle with body image

I have struggled with depression

I am an optimist

I am a dreamer and a doer

PERSONAL QUALITIES

I am a leader

I am a cheerleader for others and a natural encourager

I am real and approachable.

I am a gifted speaker

I am good on camera

I enjoy sharing my life and my story with others

I am classy

I am funny

I am dependable and reliable

I am an auntie

I have a big picture vision

I am tenacious

I have confidence

I value and lead with integrity

I love tacos

I was a competitive figure skater

I love to travel

I love adventure

I love photography

I can do accents and character voices

PROFESSIONAL QUALITIES

I am driven, focused and highly motivated

I have a clear vision for my future

I am focused on building relationships

I am unafraid of productive confrontation

I am passionate about what I do

I have a custom, system-based strategy

I have two college degrees in Communications

I have years of experience

your Connection-Based Brand to inspire others and connect with your Community.

> # "These lists are meant to empower you by looking back, so you can move forward and make the greatest impact. "

Summarizing your Gap characteristic lists are by no means intended to downplay your story, but a way to clearly define what makes you—you, and how you got here. These lists are meant to empower you by looking back, so you can move forward and make the greatest impact. But to do that, we must turn the emotional into something tangible so you can be empowered to confidently share your story when the time is right.

THE GAP
Wrap Up

I know, this was not an easy chapter, but you persevered and did the work! Even though it is a difficult process to define what makes you different, when you do, it provides such liberation when you learn who you are and give yourself permission to be you. That's what your Gap lists are for, to give you the permission and tools to be yourself.

Instead of conforming to be like someone else, finding their Gap with *The Connection Method* has allowed my clients to stand confidently in who they are and what makes them different.

James said that finding his Gap introduced him to himself.

Monica said that finding her Gap helped her embrace her ethnicity and diverse cultural background.

Elizabeth said that finding her Gap helped her own and be proud of her direct approach and personality.

Louise said that finding her Gap helped her realize that, "Being me was enough" and she could show up as herself with pride and confidence.

I hope that you learned that even though there are a lot of other people doing what you are doing, they aren't you. They don't share your story. They don't share your experiences. I hope you learned that your voice is needed. Your Gap in line is waiting to be filled by you and no one else.

Now's the time to stop running from your Gap or piggybacking on someone else's identity. Now's the time to cinch up your backpack, take a deep breath and step into your Gap in line, because there is a group of people literally waiting for you to step up, share your story and serve. Your Gap is waiting for you. Now's the time to own it.

THE GAP

In this chapter you learned:

⇨   The Gap is what makes you different.

⇨   Your story and your unique qualities and experiences have value and must be
     shared.

⇨   That there is a gap in your industry lineup with your name on it.

⇨   That the best way to serve is to step into your Gap.

⇨   That you carry a backpack full of all the little things that make you different-
     your Sasquatch Factor, that must be shared with your Community.

⇨   The three key benefits of defining your Gap.

⇨   Gives you permission to be yourself.

⇨   Provides tangible connection pieces that others can connect with

⇨   Helps you shift and maintain focus by focusing on your Community not your
     competition.

⇨   How to define your Gap and created a list of 5-10 key characteristics and
     pieces of your story that encapsulates what makes you unique.

CHAPTER EIGHT

NICHE

"We are all experts in our own little niches."

-ALEX TREBEK, TELEVISION HOST

Your Niche (pronounced: *"knee-shh"*) and your Gap are closely tied together. They work hand-in-hand to share how you're different (your Gap) and the specific area where you serve, what you specialize in, and what you are the expert in (your Niche).

In order for you to grow your Connection-Based Brand with intention, you have to get focused with what you offer. You must get specific with where you concentrate your efforts. If you spread yourself too thin trying to serve everyone in all the areas of your industry, you will create something fragile and unstable. Like a layer of thin ice on a frozen lake, when you don't have depth in a certain area, every step you take will be insecure and cautious, because you don't know when it all could break.

However, when you concentrate your efforts in a specific area, defining your Niche, it creates depth. Much like that frozen lake, when you create depth, you have something stable. You create something concrete, that can hold weight, that you can even jump on or skate on. It's solid. It confidently holds it's place.

If you can focus on creating "...something 100 people love, not something 1 million people kind of like" (Brian Chesky, co-founder of Airbnb), that's when consistency and confidence can bloom. When you focus your efforts on one area, you can stand confidently in what you've created to offer and sell, and your Community can be confident in knowing that you are the expert in this area and that they are in the best hands.

In this chapter, you will define your Niche, the specific area in your industry where you serve and/or sell, where you must focus your energy in growing and developing, the area where you are the expert (even if you don't "feel" like one).

BENEFITS OF A DEFINED NICHE

Throughout *The Connection Method*, you have worked so hard to connect with yourself, get specific with your message in order to tangibly define your Connection-Based Brand.

The Connection Method process is intended to give you clarity, the tools to stay consistent, and empower you to feel more confident in who you are and what you offer. Defining your Niche is yet another layer to help provide even more clarity, direction and intentionality as you grow.

The best part about defining your Niche, is that you don't have to "reinvent the branding wheel," per se. You have already done the hard work defining your Branding Words, Ideal Community and Gap, so in this next section, you are going to use what you have already defined to help you define your Niche.

After you have defined your Niche, you'll have even more clarity by establishing where to focus your energy and help who you most want to serve. You'll minimize confusion within your Community (and beyond) because they will know what you do and how you can help or serve them. It will be easier for people to refer you to others or recommend you for projects, since they know you are the specialist, and the expert in this area. The benefits of getting focused with your Niche are truly endless, but here are the six key benefits you will reap once you define, own and share your Niche.

BENEFIT 1: KNOW WHAT PROBLEM YOU SOLVE

In its most basic form, serving others is about solving a problem. No matter what business you own or career you're in, you are solving problems on the daily. Solving problems for your clients, team, leadership, and your closest family and friends.

Defining the specific problem and providing a solution, solidifies you as the expert in that area. Even if you don't feel like an expert (hello, Imposter Syndrome), you really are an expert (or a blossoming expert) about something. You have spent countless hours researching and gaining experience in your industry, so when you focus on, and serve in, a defined Niche, that's when your brand perception goes from generic to expert.

> " When you focus on and serve in a defined Niche, that's when your brand perception goes from generic to expert. "

If you are at the beginning of your business or career, I give you full permission to try all the things see what areas you like serving and what areas you don't. Learn about the areas in your industry, try them on for size, find what doesn't work and move on and find what does work and move in, because that is your space.

BENEFIT 2: KNOW WHERE TO FOCUS YOUR ENERGY

I've said time and time again (and I'm going to say it once more), but you only have so much time, energy, and financial resources at your disposal, so you must use them wisely. Find the specific area of your industry that energizes you and focus your efforts and resources there.

When you focus your energy on a specific area that you are passionate about, both you and your Community will be better served. When you are focused and rooted deep in a specific area, you can develop new systems and solutions to serve your Community, versus when you are spread out, scattered and unfocused, you'll just be treading water trying to stay afloat.

I remember the exact moment my life and business shifted after getting specific with my Niche. It was 2018 and I had just signed up to put together my first ever business plan and strategy with Heather Simpson of She Leads Me.

A year prior, I had made the decision to commit to my health. I lost over 50 pounds, and I witnessed firsthand how caring for my physical wellbeing directly affected my personal growth and the growth of my business. I wanted to share the message of health and share the products which helped me lose the weight, along with my photography and branding education business. I was in the mindset that I needed to empower the whole entrepreneur in every area of life!

I could do it all, right? Photography, branding education, and now ... a health expert!

It was during my business planning session that Heather asked me a question that changed the trajectory of my business forever. She asked, "Do you want to build a health business selling health products or do you want to build a 'Kelsey' business?"

I knew right then and there I needed to get focused.

My bigger vision and goals were getting sidelined by the distraction of health and wellness. Health and wellness are important, but it wasn't my message. It wasn't my purpose. My end goal was to impact my Community by giving them a chance to feel seen and heard via Connection-Based Branding education and Lifestyle Branding Photography. Health and wellness were important to me, but they were not going to be the platform from where I planted my foundation. I said goodbye to being a health guru, and said hello to my purpose, my message, my Niche, and here we are.

This book would not exist without the question Heather asked me. All of this would not have been possible without me getting specific about who I was and what I wanted to build.

If you are attached to things that don't advance you, let them go. If you're attached to a lot of different things, choose one or two and let the others go. Focus on advancing where you can best serve. Focus on advancing what you are most passionate about and what area you want to learn more and become an expert.

The need for focusing your energy is extremely applicable to you if you are connected to companies as an independent contractor (such as realtors, insurance agents, mortgage lenders and MLM's/direct sales). If you are in this space, then you need to brand you/your story/your specific offering—not theirs.

Companies and those who you partner with come and go, but your voice and vision remain. Build your Niche and overall brand message based on your Connection-Based Brand, not theirs. Build what you specialize in so it can go with you wherever you go.

Ask yourself, "Do you want to build _____ (your affiliate company's name) _____ brand/business or do you want to build a ____ (your name)____ business/brand?"

yes

branding *you*

no

branding *them*

yes

branding *you*

no

branding *them*

For example:

Do you want to build a Rodan and Fields business or do you want to build a ____ (insert your name) ____ business?

Do you want to build a doTERRA business or do you want to build a ____ (insert your name) ____ business?

Do you want to build a Sotheby's Real Estate business or do you want to build a ____ (insert your name) ____ business?

Do you want to build a State Farm Insurance business or do you want to build a ____ (insert your name) ____ business?

BENEFIT 3: ATTRACT THE RIGHT PEOPLE

Your Niche adds another layer to your Attract List by identifying even further who you serve and the problems you can solve for your Community. You already know the characteristics and demographics of who you want to attract, so defining your Niche helps you narrow down even further the specific Community you can serve.

BENEFIT 4: MINIMIZE CONFUSION

One of the most common phrases in the branding and marketing word is, "A confused mind always says no." The original author of this quote is unknown, but the truth is sound.

If your Community doesn't know what to expect or what you do, they are going to run from the unknown. If you ask me what I do and answer, "Well, I'm a photographer. I take pictures of all sorts of stuff. You know, whatever gets thrown my way," you're going to run the other direction. Especially if you are a potential client looking to have professional photos taken. That answer is not professional or builds confidence in their perception of my abilities to capture them well.

However, if I respond with "I am a Lifestyle Branding Photographer who specializes in going beyond the headshot to illustrates the heart of your business in order to maximize client connection and trust," you're going feel confident and not confused knowing who I am and what area I specifically serve.

Simplify your offering and become an expert in that area. That way, your Community can easily understand what you do and how you can serve them. Keep it focused. Keep it simple.

BENEFIT 5: SIMPLIFY REFERRALS

I have two basic rules for business, 1) make it easy for people to give you money and 2) make it easy for people to refer you.

One of the most common goals business owners and leaders share is that they want to remain at the top of mind when their Community is looking for someone to serve them in their industry, hire them or even being considered for a promotion or new opportunity.

When you get specific about what you offer, your Community will consider you as their personal expert in that area. So, when your area of expertise comes up in conversations, your name will be thrown into discussion along with a glowing anecdote of how great you are!

When you define and commit to your Niche, it makes it simple for your Ideal Community to find you, connect with you, hire you and most importantly *refer* you to others in their circle.

BENEFIT 6: PROVIDES A WAY TO SHARE YOUR GAP + STORY

Defining your Niche provides a way to share not only what you do but why you do it. It provides a way to share how you are different (your Gap) both personally and professionally. Your Niche opens the door to connection by sharing more of who you are, what you value, and what people can expect from you.

Take, for example, a friend who is a divorce mediator. She explained that in her line of work she is used to being hated. She works with people during one of the most stressful, emotional, and fearful times in their lives, so she truly witnesses the worst in people. However, despite sometimes being hated by one party or another, she genuinely loves what she does.

After going through a messy and complex divorce herself, she wanted to offer a different approach and desired to make the process better. She was motivated by her own experience and wanted to provide a different approach to the divorce process.

Yes, she specializes in divorce mediation services, that is her Niche, but she is motivated by her own story, her own experiences (her Gap) which fuels her desire to help people streamline the process by minimizing unnecessary financial and emotional turmoil. She used her Gap and story as a compass to help her focus in on what area she wanted to serve others in and become their expert for navigating their divorce.

DEFINE YOUR NICHE: THE QUESTIONS

Now it's time to answer the questions to help you define your Niche. These questions will help you define two areas of your Niche; where you are most passionate in your industry, and where you are least passionate in your industry. These questions are meant to help you get focused and create a deep and intentional Niche that you can grow and build on in the years to come.

QUESTION SET 1 OF 2: NICHE BASICS

1. **Do you currently have a defined Niche? Do you currently have something you specialize in?**
    If so, share it with me! Could you get even more specific? Are there other areas you could grow within this Niche? If you don't, no problem-o! Proceed to the next question!

2. **What are the *3-5 biggest problems* you solve?**
    Think about the pain points or challenges you defined in the Branding Words and Ideal Community sections. Expand on them. Also, think beyond the product or service you sell. Look at the heart of what you do, why do people need you, your product/ service in their life?

3. **What area(s) in your industry are you most passionate about?**

   Think about the clients, jobs or opportunities that light your fire and you get the most excited about serving.

4. **Consider your answer to the previous question, are these specific areas of your industry ones you are truly passionate about and could see yourself developing for the next 5 years?**

   In order to develop and grow your Niche expertise, it takes time, consistency, and work to get there. Be sure you are identifying areas in your industry that you could spend time growing over the next 5 + years.

5. **What area(s) in your industry are you *least* passionate about?**

   Think about the clients, jobs or opportunities that drain you and extinguish your fire and excitement. What people, projects or areas within your industry do you groan and roll your eyes at? What areas or opportunities would you feel good about passing onto someone else?

6. **Are there any areas that you need to consider letting go of, hiring out for, or passing the opportunity to someone else?**

7. **What is your "competition" *NOT* providing?**

   Look back to your notes and answers from the Gap section. Think about others in your industry. What are they not providing? (ex: non authentic branding, dishonest or non-transparent services, not professional, nonspecific offering, not providing quality value, etc.)

QUESTION SET 2 OF 2: EXPERTISE

You are an expert at something. You may not feel like one, but you have spent more time than the average person learning, growing, and honing your skills in a certain area. You're developing your place as an expert.

You may be wondering, "What's so special about what I do?" But take my word, you are exceptional, and what you do is extraordinary. Even if it seems basic and simple, your Community wants to learn and tap into what you have to offer, so let's define your expertise!

1. **What initially attracted you to this business/profession?**
   Go back to the beginning and think about why you started. Was it a calling? Was it money? Was it passion? Was it education? Was it convenience?

2. **Why are you still in your business/profession?**
   What keeps you doing what you do every day? Do you wake up with excitement or dread in the mornings?

3. **What skill/topic would you consider yourself an EXPERT at?**
   An "expert" is defined as someone who has devoted an extensive

amount of time and passion learning, honing, and growing in a specific area of study or skill set. Go ahead, tell me why you are really good at what you do!

4. **Why would you consider yourself an EXPERT in this skill/topic/job?**
Think about your education, experience, passion, research, collaboration etc. Why does this skill/topic/job light your fire? It's ok, brag on yourself!

5. **How do you feel about your area of expertise? And why?**
Confident, proud, ashamed, excited, hesitant, need more growth, like a "fraud" or insecure? Do you want to continue growing this specific area expertise? Change course?

6. **In one or two sentences, what you ultimately want to do in your business/profession.**
Are you doing it now? If not, what would it take to ultimately get to where you want to go?

DEFINE YOUR NICHE: SUMMARIZE

Go back through your answers and note any repetitive words or phrases. Identify two areas:

⇨ Your passion zone

⇨ Your passionless zone

LIST ONE:
PASSION ZONE

Write down the areas where you are most passionate about. Is it working with first time homebuyers, mentoring up-and-coming artists, luxury weddings and events, first time parents, high level athletes, natural health, special effects makeup artistry, technical education, self-help for corporate leaders, etc.

Find 1-3 areas within your industry you are most passionate about advancing. Ideally, it's best to focus your energy on just one or two areas, but a third can be added in if it has direct ties to your Niche.

Look back at what you said you are most passionate about and make this your focus. Let your excitement and energy fuel your growth within that specific area. Make sure that Niche this is something that you could see yourself pursuing and growing for the next 5+ years.

Use your Passion Zone list and finish the following statements:

I am most passionate about ....
I am energized most by helping ...
I enjoy learning and educating others about ...

Your answers to the above statements will be your Niche statements. They will provide the direction for you to know where you should focus giving your energy and attention. They will be the area(s) in which you will become the expert or continue growing as the expert in your industry.

LIST TWO:
PASSION-LESS ZONE

Investing time into areas you are not passionate or energized about will keep you feeling spread too thin, scattered, insecure and not confident in what you offer. It's time to let go and focus on serving within your Passion Zone, in your Niche.

If you aren't passionate about a certain area of your industry that you are currently offering, let it go! Shift your work, business, and career to something that energizes you. If you are doing things that are a part of your job, but take your attention away from serving within your Niche (like social media management, website building or administrative tasks), let it go and hire someone.

If you say yes to opportunities that you're not passionate about, are not within your Niche, or don't align with your overall Connection-Based Brand message, let them go! When you say yes to something outside of your Niche, it confuses your Community, takes your energy and focus away from the work you should be doing. By say saying yes to something outside of your Niche, it takes the opportunity away from someone who is passionate about that area.

> " By say saying yes to something outside of
> your Niche, it takes the opportunity away from
> someone who is passionate about that area. "

By saying yes to this, it inspires doubt, confusion, distraction and diminishes the growth of your overall industry by preventing others the chance to add their skills and talents to the mix which up levels the industry for all.

Dump what drains you and invest your time energy and resources into building your Niche and building your place as the expert within that space.

Use your Passion-less Zone list and finish the following statements:

⇨ I am least passionate about ...

⇨ I don't enjoy learning about or educating others about ...

⇨ I need to let go of ....

⇨ When I let go of (insert above answer) I will have more time for

NICHE
Wrap Up

Simplifying your offering to just the things you are passionate and committed to will help you build consistency and become the expert. Defining your Niche gives you permission to not have to do it all, but instead invites you to create a specific offering that solves the problems of and serves those in your Ideal Community.

Your Niche helps direct where you need to spend your precious time, energy and resources as well as attracting the people who energize you, appreciate you and advance your goals and vision. Your Niche also helps to minimize confusion about what you do, which provides a simple way for others to remember who you are, how you serve and easily refer you to others.

Chapter Recap

NICHE

In this chapter you learned:

⇨ **What is a Niche?**

⇨ **The six benefits of a defined Niche**

1. Know what problem you solve
2. Know where to focus your energy
3. Attract the right people
4. Minimize confusion
5. Simplify referrals
6. Provides a way to share your Gap and story

⇨ **The questions to ask in order to define your Niche**

⇨ **How to define your Niche**

⇨ **Define your Passion Zone**

⇨ **Define your Passion-less Zone**

CHAPTER NINE

VALUE PROPOSITION

"If you can't write your message in a sentence,
you can't say it in an hour."

-Dianna Booher, Author & Communications Consultant

Have you ever encountered that moment when someone asks, "What do you do?" And just like a startled goat, you freeze in terror, your legs lock up, and you feel like you're going to tip over as your brain decides to leave your body and take a spontaneous vacation to the beach.

Once you regain consciousness, you begin the laborious attempt to answer the question and begin to ramble off random facts and stories about who you are, what you do or why they should care. You end up down a rabbit hole telling a ridiculously long story about your barista's roommate's cousin, who was the one who introduced you to your industry

10 years ago while at a fishing derby in Seward, Alaska where you caught a 200-pound Halibut.

Yep, I'm exhausted by that story too, but we've all been there and fallen prey to the Word Vomit Monster.

This scenario is quite common and something we all experience. For most of the human population, it is extremely difficult to talk about ourselves in a confident and intentional way.

However, ask us about our favorite bakery, we can gush all day about their crispy, yet soft and seemingly orgasmic donuts. Ask us about who we love to follow on Instagram, and we will give you a categorical list of why we connect with their feed. Ask us about our hairdresser, and we will tell you, in intricate detail, why they are a miracle worker. Ask us about anything other than ourselves, and we can show up and discuss it. But when it's about us? Hell to the no.

So, in order to avoid the petrified goat scenario, or rambling on for 45 minutes trying to explain what we do, we are going to tackle this topic head on. You will use all of the branding elements you have defined in the previous chapters to create a go-to, powerhouse, knock 'em dead, statement, so when you are hit with the "What do you do?" question, you are prepared with exactly what to say.

This statement is called your Value Proposition.

Your Value Proposition is simply how you communicate your Connection-Based Brand message.

Instead of blehhh-ing all over people with random words and stories, you'll show up as the confident badass that you are, telling them exactly who you are and how you serve.

Instead of trying to come up with something new to say every time, you'll have a foundational statement that is consistent with your brand message and can be customized to fit any situation. Your Value Proposition is your intentional and consistent answer to the "What do you do?" question.

DITCH THE ELEVATOR PITCH

Traditionally, the answer to "What do you do?" has been commonly referred to as an elevator pitch. A phrase that you can quickly tell someone in an elevator traveling between floors. However, I have always loathed this phrase with deep animosity.

Whenever I heard the phrase, elevator pitch, I would cringe. I would imagine standing in front of elevator doors, and as the doors open, inside are a group of old white men in suits, holding briefcases. They look at me and say with sweet condescension, "Well, hi, little lady! What can you do for us, kiddo? What are you going to try and sell us? How can we improve your life by saying yes to your little offering?"

This visual makes me both annoyed and angry at the same time since it conveys a message that I must prove who I am and my offering is worthy of their oh-so precious time and attention. It undermines the experience and value I and my business bring to the table.

I don't know about you, but no matter your gender, that type of scenario is never empowering.

Being the little rebel that I am, I sought a new perspective. I decided that *The Connection Method* would take you down a different path. A path that would communicate what you do through a different approach. An approach not out of desperation, but one of value.

Instead of an elevator pitch, you will develop your *Value Proposition*. This statement not only tells your Community who you are and what you do, but communicates it by actively using your Branding Words, attracting your Ideal Community, repelling the wrong people, and presenting the solutions and values you bring to the table. This statement will share value, connect with your audience, and leave them wanting more. This statement is your core tool for sharing your Connection-Based Brand message with the world, and is the first spark of establishing connections with others.

Sounds amazing, right?

Developing this statement is no cake walk. It takes a lot of trial and error as it evolves. It takes time to navigate how to put the words together, keep them in your voice, and be able to seamlessly share it out loud. It takes time, but the good news is you have already done the leg work by defining the critical elements needed to create your Value Proposition. Your Branding Words along with your Ideal Community, Gap and Niche will help you create this statement.

Defining your Value Proposition is the fifth and final step of *The Connection Method* process. This is the time where you put everything you have defined together into this seemingly magical, unicorn sneeze, rainbow dust explosion type of statement. You have the tools, now, let's build it.

WHAT IS A VALUE PROPOSITION?

The term Value Proposition is a marketing buzzword traditionally used to describe the first statement visitors see on your website. It's the statement that quickly tells people who you are, why you are different, and why they should keep scrolling down your site to learn more.

Now, to be clear, a Value Proposition is not a mission statement or a tagline. Mission statements focus inward on a person or business, conveying the purpose or the specific goals of a business or individual. A tagline is a quick, punchline, catchphrase or slogan used mainly for outreach and advertising purposes.

Your Value Proposition is there to help you quickly and effectively communicate what you do, and it is for others to quickly learn how you could enrich their life, provide value and solve their problem(s).

Effective Value Propositions are created how your Ideal Community would describe what you do, not how you describe what you do.

Value Propositions are free from industry specific jargon and use simple, brand consistent terminology to easily inform, attract, and excite the right people. Your Value Proposition is about telling the world how you are different, what you specialize in and how you add value to others. Your Value Proposition is for them, not you. Keep it simple and to the point.

VALUE PROPOSITION: THE EQUATION

Below is the equation I've cooked up to help you patch your Value Proposition together. It is intended to help you take all the elements of your brand and summarize them down into a one or two sentence statement.

Keep in mind that this is not a hard fast equation and can be customized to work with how you wish to communicate your brand message. The most important thing is to organize your thoughts to make a statement that is simple, clear, easy to comprehend and leaves them wanting more.

Just like a good mystery novel, you don't want to give it all away in the first two sentences. Don't overload your Value Proposition, this statement is intended just to give a taste of what you do. It is meant to inform, but also intrigue and entice your audience to go beyond the initial conversation (or digital interaction) and seek more information and connection.

This is the Value Proposition equation. It will help you formulate an intentional answer to "what do you do?"

When developing your Value Proposition, your Branding Words lead the way. Your Branding Words are the starting point and framework for the statement. Your Branding Words may be enough to convey the full phrase, or you may need to add other branding elements to it as well. You gauge how it develops, but let your Branding Words take the lead.

A great way to start brainstorming your Value Proposition is to finish the sentence "I help ..." or "I create ..." or "I lead ..." or "I provide ..." then insert your Branding Words and/or other branding elements. We'll work on this more after you review the following examples.

VALUE PROPOSITION: EXAMPLES

Value Propositions are complex things to create, so I wanted to give you plenty of examples of what different Value Propositions look like. I've shared the industry, their Branding Words, and the Value Proposition(s) they use to answer the question "What do you do?"

DIRECT SALES REPRESENTATIVE (SKIN CARE)

Branding Words: Confidence, Care, Innovative, Community, Integrity

Value Proposition: "I help others feel confident in their own skin and business by providing care and support through our community and innovative products"

BOUDOIR PHOTOGRAPHER

Branding Words: Transformative, Luxurious, Connection, Judgement-Free, Leader

Value Proposition: "Leading my clients through a transformative luxurious experience in a safe space that allows them to connect with themselves and see their true beauty"

HEALTH COACH

Branding Words: Transparency, Solutions, Progressive, Advocate, Passion

Value Proposition: "I am a progressive health coach who passionately advocates for you to find real solutions for you to sleep better, feel better, weigh less and improve mental health."

FOOD BLOGGER

Branding Words: Bold, Fresh, Innovative, Passion, Real

Value Proposition: "I help real people get inspired to cook bold and fresh food."

PROFESSIONAL ORGANIZER

Branding Words: Luxury, Calm, Simple, Relatable, Non-Judgmental

Value Proposition: "We create luxurious calm by simplifying your home and life."

SOCIAL MEDIA MARKETER

Branding Words: Community, Empower, Resource, Accessible, Dependable

Value Proposition(s): I provide social media services that create community, save you time and empower you to grow your small businesses in Seattle and beyond!

"Social media management for small business looking to simplify marketing by maximizing their results."

MORTGAGE LENDER 1

Branding Words: Connection, Communication, Care, Commitment, Clarity

Value Proposition: "Offering a clear, effective and caring approach to your mortgage experience."

MORTGAGE LENDER 2

Branding Words: Leader, Solutions, Confidence, Excellence, Edgy Fun

Value Proposition: "Leading you through the mortgage process with confidence, experience, custom solutions ... and a little unexpected fun along the way."

RETAIL MANAGER

Branding Words: Dependable, Driven, Leader, Creative, Compassion

Value Proposition: "I am a dependable leader who seeks out opportunities to provide creative solutions and care for others."

INSURANCE AGENT

Branding Words: Passionate, Honest, Educator, Enthusiastic, Protect

Value Proposition: "I'm a personal insurance agent who is passionate about building true and honest relationships while helping achievers and leaders protect their lifestyle and legacy."

SPECIAL EVENT PERFORMANCE GROUP

Branding Words: Magical, Fantasy, Excellence, Diverse, Trust

Value Proposition: "Providing magical entertainment for family, corporate and community events. You will experience magical moments and leave with unforgettable memories."

HAIR + AESTHETICS SALON

Branding Words: Community, Confidence, Consistent, Modern, Trust

Value Proposition: "We help women rediscover their confidence through skin, hair and body care. We are passionate about giving women a place where they feel like they belong."

REALTOR 1

Branding Words: Creative, Bold, Community, Excellence, Joy

Value Proposition: "Creative real estate solutions connecting you to your dream home and community."

REALTOR 2

Branding Words: Integrity, Relationships, Resource, Tenacious

Value Proposition: "Integrity-led realtor focused on education, building relationships and fighting for you to help you reach your goals in real estate."

REAL ESTATE BROKERAGE (CORPORATE)

Branding Words: Community, Collaboration, Connection, Craft, Culture

Value Proposition: "Community-led brokerage focused on supporting brokers through a collaborative culture and crafted education."

VALUE PROPOSITION: THE PROCESS

Now that you can see what is possible, let's get to work defining your Value Proposition. Please have your finalized Branding Words, Ideal Community, Gap Characteristics and Niche on hand. You'll use these to build and validate your Value Proposition. Before we hop into it, let's take a look at the Value Proposition Equation, one more time:

STEP 1: REVIEW + COMPILE

Review each of your branding elements. First look at your Branding Words. They lead the way to where your Value Proposition starts and how it develops. Next, use your other branding elements (Ideal Community, Attract List, Demographic, Gap, and Niche) to give you inspiration and summarize even further. Feel free to look back at the examples for inspiration and guidance.

To get you started, use the sentence prompts below. Choose one that feels right to you and roll with it. During this process, don't be afraid to speak your ideas out loud like you are talking to someone. Verbally expressing ideas can help your voice come out more naturally.

"I help ..."

"I create ..."

"I lead ..."

"I provide ..."

"I (Branding Word) ..."

"(Branding Word/Core Value)-led ..."

STEP 2: WORKSHOP YOUR PROP

The next step is to take your Value Proposition rough draft, and grab a trusted/honest friend, and some snacks, because it's time to workshop your Prop! This is the time to get out of your head and start to actively speak your Value Proposition with real people.

Speaking your Value Proposition out loud is the only way for it to sound like you, and not like a robot. Find a friend who is nonjudgmental, yet not afraid to give you constructive criticism, who can critically think with you, and ideally someone who doesn't know the full ins and outs of what you do.

Read your rough Value Proposition out loud to your friend, and then ask the following questions:

⇨ "From what I just said, what do you think I do?"

⇨ "What value do you think I bring?"

⇨ "Was this statement ME focused or OTHERS focused?" (You want your audience to feel like you can help them, not just feeding your ego by telling them how great you are without providing value)

⇨ "Was this a clear statement or confusing? Was there any terminology that didn't make sense?"

⇨ "What part resonated with you the most?"

⇨ "What suggestions do you have to improve this to flow better and sound like me?"

WORKSHOP YOUR PROP + SHARE:

I would love it if you would share your workshopping experience with the Connection Crew on Social Media! Take photos or share stories of your Value Proposition workshop experience so we can cheer you on!

Use the hashtag: #TheConnectionMethod

STEP 3: COMMIT TO IMPERFECT

After workshopping your Value Proposition with a friend, work through the changes you discussed and then commit to your imperfect Value Proposition statement. Yes, it is imperfect, and will be a continual work in progress until you have actively used it out in the real world.

Don't stress that you must have your Value Proposition all figured out or have it perfect before you can start using it. Having a perfect Value Proposition right from the start is like having a rare purple peach growing in the Yukon. It's unlikely and not the expectation. This process takes time. So, breathe, and know that time will only make this statement and your confidence applying it stronger and stronger.

VALUE PROPOSITION
Wrap Up

Bravo! You're a total badass! You just did a ton of work!

I know you may still have questions or wonder if what you have defined is good enough, but I assure you, it is! Your Value Proposition will take time to evolve and feel natural, so keep working on it, practice speaking it, and give yourself grace!

Your Value Proposition is not meant for you to spew out all at once. It's there so you have the go-to keywords and phrases at the ready to communicate with others effectively and consistently, and naturally weave into conversations or in your digital presence. Your Value Proposition serves as the baseline for communicating with others your brand message and how you can serve them.

Your Value Proposition is the final branding piece of *The Connection Method*. Think about where you started at the beginning of this process. You came to this book feeling scattered and needing direction. You came to this book wanting to learn about the possibilities of defining a Connection-Based Brand. And you did. By doing the hard work and connecting with yourself, you are now able to connect with others genuinely, intentionally, and effectively.

You now have a consistent and tangible brand that defines the narrative of who you are and what you offer. Instead of letting others tell you who you are, you have taken the power back and are able to tell others who you are and how they should speak about you. You can now confidently proclaim, "This is me! I am proud of who I am and am so ready to serve you with my unique gifts, story and offering! Let's go!"

Way to slay this section, my friend. You have done incredible work and are rapidly on your way to creating a Brand Legacy and stepping out as a Connection-Based Leader.

VALUE PROPOSIITON

In this chapter you learned:

⇨ What a Value Proposition is and is not

⇨ The Value Proposition Equation

⇨ Examples of Value Propositions

⇨ Ideas and prompts for creating your Value Proposition

⇨ How to workshop and implement your Value Proposition

⇨ Confirmation that you are a BADASS!

CHAPTER TEN

THE 5 CORE FEARS

"The fears we don't face become our limits."
-Robin Sharma, Author

When I was midway in my photography career, I arrived at an inevitable time every business owner faces … having to raise my prices.

I had been offering full photography services for weddings and portraits for over 5 years, but at 50% below the average market rate. Even though my skill set, community awareness, and offering had grown tremendously in this time, my pricing had barely changed since I started my business. It hadn't changed because I was afraid of losing clients if I charged too much. It hadn't changed because I was afraid of looking greedy and selfish.

Then one day, I had a conversation with a potential marketing partner, and after looking at my rates she said, "Kelsey, you are one of the best photographers in the area, but your rates tell me that you are one of the worst. For us to work together, your rates need to match your work, otherwise we can't do business."

What she said felt like a direct punch to the gut.

It was a truth bomb, and it was nuclear, but I needed to hear it. It helped me get out of my head and realize there are more people involved in my business and career than just me. These people want to hire me and pay me what I'm worth. They are just waiting for me to get out of my own way so they can support me.

After that conversation, I decided to take my pricing seriously and *tripled my rate*. It made me want to vomit.

Fear started swirling in my head. "No one will pay this!" "My business will collapse!" "I feel bad taking people's money!" "I'm not good enough to charge this amount!" And on and on the self-doubt continued to swirl.

I remember going into my first wedding consultation with my new prices. When it was time to go over pricing and packages, my stomach was in knots as I told them how much it would be. And without batting an eye, they chose my largest package.

They said they were so excited to work with me and that my pricing was equivalent to the other pro-level photographers they were considering. They said my pricing and services made them feel more confident that they were getting someone high quality and someone who they could trust to care for them and their big day.

I was flabbergasted, and I started to realize that maybe raising my prices wasn't a bad idea after all. This same scenario happened every single time with wedding clients, and eventually as I shifted my focus to Lifestyle Branding photography, it followed the same pattern. My Community saw the unique and empowering experience I offered and the quality work I offered, and they were willing to pay for it.

Because I started valuing myself, valuing my time and my talent, I started attracting clients who genuinely appreciated what I offered vs taking advantage of me. I worked less for more and was working with intention and direction, not out of desperation and impulsivity.

Offering a professional service paired with professional rates opened so many incredible opportunities. I was able to travel internationally, work on beautiful projects, speak to incredible groups, and connect with people who perfectly matched my Ideal Community Attract List. My Community was waiting at my doorstep ready for me to serve them, I just had to get out of my own way, I had to get past my own fears.

The only thing that was holding me back from the life, business, career, and Community I truly desired was fear. The same fear that may be holding you back. In this chapter, we are going to dive into the Five Core Fears which will be waiting for you as you step out and share your Connection-Based Brand out in the real world.

YOU DEFINED THE BRAND, NOW DEFINE THE FEAR

In the previous chapters, you have defined an incredibly powerful and unique to you Connection-Based Brand.

However, even if you have the most perfectly curated Connection-Based Brand, fear is the biggest thing preventing you from going out and sharing it. You are stepping out from behind the traditional idea of branding by hiding behind a logo or business card and putting yourself out there. You. For all the world to see. When you step out with your story and your Connection-Based Brand message, fear, insecurity, second guessing, immobility, what-ifs, and anxiety will be waiting to latch on, so we can't ignore it. Fear must be addressed. Fear must be defined.

No matter the role you hold as an entrepreneur, business owner or a leader, everything is tied back to you as the human behind the brand. You are the deciding factor whether or not your business or career takes off or withers away.

In order to be equipped for what's waiting for you after you press the launch button of your Connection-Based Brand, you must also define your fears, the things that can and will pop up to prevent you from stepping out, taking action, and making the impact you want to make.

Just like defining your Connection-Based Brand, when you can define fear, the fear transforms from being an abstract emotion into something tangible that you can process and manage versus feeling out of control, scattered or immobilized.

After working with countless entrepreneurs and leaders over the years, I started hearing similar stories about fear and what was holding them back from stepping out. What was holding them back from sharing their Connection-Based Brand and holding them back from stepping up to the next level of success?

I heard all the fears. The big ones, the little ones, the specific ones, and even the subconscious ones, and I noticed that they all had similar qualities. I realized that every one of the fears I heard could be summarized into *Five Core Fears*.

Please note, that this next section is not an attempt to trivialize deep rooted fears or dismiss them in anyway. It is meant to be an awareness tool and tangible process you can use to help you recognize the fear so you take the power back.

" You are in the driver's seat, not fear. "

This chapter is intended to help you take the emotional fear and turn it into something tangible. To have your fear give you power instead of paralysis. When you have that power, you are in the driver's seat, not fear. And when you are in the driver's seat, you get to determine the route and how fast you go. Versus fear, who always pushes the breaks and keeps you immobile, worrying and overthinking on the side of the road.

THE 5 CORE FEARS

Imagine a plot of land with five houses on it. To get to each house, there are seemingly an infinite number of winding paths, trails, roads, and detours all leading to a specific house. Those paths are our personal fears.

When we are on a path it feels overwhelming, alone, heavy with anxiety and confusion, but if we look up from the jumbled path, we can see that each of these paths connect to something bigger. Connected to a source, to one of the Five Core Fears.

Just like defining your Connection-Based Brand, when you can step out of the emotional and turn it into something tangible by defining your Core Fear, you regain clarity, and you take back your power. That way, instead of being paralyzed with fear and letting fear stall your goals, you can move forward with making an impact with your Connection-Based Brand and serving your Community.

The Five Core Fears are:

5 core fears

CORE FEAR 1. Fear of Others' Opinions

CORE FEAR 2. Fear of Failure or Success

CORE FEAR 3. Fear of Disappointment

CORE FEAR 4. Fear of Inadequacy

CORE FEAR 5. Fear of The Unknown

CORE FEAR 1:
FEAR OF OTHERS' OPINIONS

"Those who tell you that you cannot fly are the ones who chained themselves to the ground."

- SAI PRADEEP, AUTHOR

"What will people say if I start my own business?"

"What will people think if I go after a promotion?"

"What will people think if I put myself out there on social media?"

"What will they say if I fail?"

"What if they say no and reject me?"

"What if I make a fool of myself?"

"What will they say if I really tell them how I'm doing?"

"If I show my true self, will people even like me anymore?"

The Fear of Other's Opinions is one of the most common fears humans have, and especially common among individuals who are in a leadership position. Leaders who put themselves out there with their Connection-Based Brand are especially susceptible to this fear. The Fear of Others' Opinions is also linked to common fears such as being judged, rejection, humiliation, and of being perceived as selfish or narcissistic.

Many of our Connection Crew community say that The Fear of Others' Opinions is one of the core reasons they don't put themselves out there or go after bigger goals. They're afraid of how their actions will come across or that they will be rejected or judged by their peers and community.

Your secret weapon for reclaiming your power is your Connection-Based Brand.

When you have a defined Connection-Based Brand, YOU define the narrative. You are the one who tells others how they should perceive you and speak about you.

> " When you have a defined Connection-Based Brand, YOU define the narrative. You are the one who tells others how they should perceive you and speak about you. "

The longer you stay consistent in your brand message, your Community will start speaking your Branding Words and brand message back to you.

For example, my Branding Words are *Real, Education, Inspiration, Empower and Joy.* The messages and comments I receive or conversations I have sound something like this …

"I love how REAL you are."

"Your Instagram stories brought me so much JOY today!"

"I LEARN so much from you."

"You INSPIRE me to take initiative."

"I feel so much more EMPOWERED now after defining my brand."

I share these messages to illustrate the power that *your* Connection-Based Brand has to define the narrative. The power your Connection-Based Brand has to lead your Community by sharing how you want them to see you and speak about you. You may or may not broadcast your Branding Words publicly, but once you commit to living them , your Community will pick up the message and speak about you the way you have defined yourself—not them.

When you do own and fully commit to sharing your Connection-Based Brand narrative, it doesn't mean you are immune to fear and judgment. It's not if, but when someone has an opinion about you.

It is up to you to choose where to give your energy and focus. Will you concentrate your energy on the negative person or small group of people who don't believe in you or respect you (your Repel Listers)? Or will you give your energy to the people who truly appreciate you and what you have to offer (your Attract Listers). You can't please everyone, so focus on speaking to and serving your Ideal Community. They are primed and excited to support you.

When you find yourself wondering "What will people say about me?" or "What will people think about me," remember, your Connection-Based Brand is right there in the corner of the boxing ring ready to go in and fight for you. You define the narrative. Not them.

FEAR OF OTHERS' OPINIONS: QUESTIONS

You didn't think you would get out of this section without answering a few questions, did you? This is *The Connection Method* after all where I ask all the questions! So, let's dig deeper into this fear. If the Fear of Others' Opinions is something you struggle with or want to dig deeper into,, process and answer the questions below.

1. **On a scale of 1-10 how affected are you by The Fear of Others' Opinions?**

   1: people's opinions don't matter to me - 10: terrified/it holds me back.

2. **What opinion do you fear the most?**

   Fear of people thinking bad about you? People judging you? People rejecting you? People thinking you are self-involved? People making fun of you? Fear of ...?

3. **Identify the people in your life whose opinions mean the most to you.**

   Are they family? Friends? Clients? Your Team? Your leadership? Random people?

4. **Why do their opinions matter so much to you?**

   Why do their opinions affect you so much?

5. **If those people had a bad opinion of you, what would you do?**

   How would you feel?

6. **If those people had a positive opinion of you, what would you do?**

   How would you feel?

7. **How much time in a day do you spend thinking about others' opinions of you?**

8. **How much time in a day do you think others spend thinking about you?**

9. **What would you set out to do if you knew it was 100% guaranteed that whatever you did people would have a positive opinion about you/what you're doing?**

10. **If you DON'T feel or experience the Fear of Others' Opinions, why do you think that is?**

    Think about why this fear doesn't strongly affect you. Is it your personal or professional history? Your personality? Your value set? Your mindset? Define why this isn't a noteworthy fear for you.

CORE FEAR 2:
FEAR OF FAILURE OR SUCCESS

"Doubt kills more dreams than failure ever will."

- *Suzy Kassem, Author*

I've cheated in school. I've been homeless. I've had to use the foodbank. I got divorced at 32. I've lied. I have gained back the weight I'd lost. I've made poor choices with money. I've hurt the ones I love. I've made mistakes in my business. I have not come through for people when they needed me. I have failed.

You are reading a book authored by a big-fat-failure.

Nevertheless, my shortcomings as a human didn't stop me from moving forward. The one thing I know for certain is that *failure is inevitable*. It's not *if* you will fail, but *when*. There is no way to avoid it.

Arianna Huffington's voice pops up in my head when I am facing failure head on. She says, "Failure is not the opposite of success, it's part of success."

Knowing that failure is a part of the success process validates that we are moving in the right direction. I promise you; you will encounter some type of failure. Don't think of failure as failure, think of failure as redirection. A direct nudge for you to reevaluate and change course.

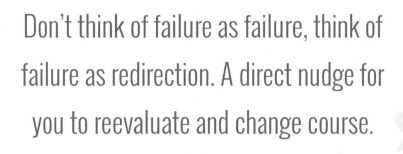

> " Don't think of failure as failure, think of failure as redirection. A direct nudge for you to reevaluate and change course. "

A woman in our Connection Crew Community shared with me that she wanted to go back to school and start a new career. However, she was terrified that if she did, she would fail. She was afraid of getting in over her head, not performing well at her studies and wasting time and money. All she could see was a big neon sign blinking, "You're a failure" ... even before she took any action.

Fear blinded her, so she couldn't see the bigger picture. When you think about starting something new or building on what you have already created, the only perspective you have to base your decision on, is your own *current perspective*.

She couldn't see the people she would meet and the friendships she would create, the opportunities that would present themselves, or the things she would learn if she went for it. She couldn't see the respect she would receive, the confidence that would build, or the lives she would touch. Based on her current reality, and before taking any action, she pre-decided that her dreams were a lost cause. She pre-decided she was failure. She let her fear determine her future, without even taking a step forward and making an attempt at trying something different.

If you are susceptible to The Fear of Failure, the thing that will help you combat this fear is staying consistent in your Connection-Based Brand

and a little splash of faith. Staying consistent gives you the actionable steps to put one foot in front of the other, while faith helps maintain your inner dialog of "What if?"

Consistency and faith that your decision to step into scary things will pay off—even when you don't know the outcome, or the outcome ends up not what you expected, in the end you will have forward progress versus being frozen in time with fear.

The Fear of Failure also has a fraternal twin sister named Fear of Success. These two fears may not look alike, but they have the same genetic baseline from where the fear power is created.

Fear of Failure is assumption based and punishing yourself when you haven't achieved the things you assumed you should achieve. Fear of Success is fearing how others react to your achievement. For those who struggle with the Fear of Success, the pressure to maintain this level of success is daunting.

One of my friends who was a high-level athlete in college explained to me that she called the Fear of Success, her "fear of being great." She said that she was "...worried that if I work at my 100%, it will always be expected ... and I'm not sure I want to do that. Growing up playing sports, I feared the pressure of what being incredibly good would bring. I love pushing myself and love crushing goals, but I want to do it at my pace."

The symptoms of the Fear of Success show itself as setting low goals, not taking opportunities, perfectionism, procrastination, bowing out of projects prematurely, or fear that others will think of you as above them or self-involved.

Whether you struggle with The Fear of Failure or The Fear of Success, when you can learn to be proud of both your failure and success, you are able to grow and move forward towards your goals, and in turn, connect even deeper with your Ideal Community.

By being vulnerable and showing your failures, your Community can feel seen. By showing your successes, they can celebrate with you, witness it can be done, and feel a part of something bigger. Both your failures and successes are win-win scenarios, and a reminder that what you are doing has a greater purpose and impact for both yourself and your Community.

FEAR OF FAILURE OR SUCCESS: QUESTIONS

If the Fear of Failure or Fear of Success is something you struggle with or want to dig deeper into, process and answer the following questions.

1. **Define failure. What does failure look like?**
   If you "failed" at something what would that life look like? Be specific.

2. **Think about the failure you described above, what would you do if that happened to you?**
   Would you give up? Would you fight? Would you ask for help? How would you respond?

3. **Define success. What does success look like?**
   If you "succeeded" what would that life look like? Be specific.

4. **Think about the success you described above, what would you do if that happened to you?**

   Would you downplay it and set lower goals? Would you be self-conscious? Would you be proud of yourself? Would you go bigger? Would you maintain? How would you respond?

5. **If you DON'T feel or experience the Fear of Failure or the Fear of Success, why do you think that is?**

   Think about why this fear doesn't strongly affect you. Is it your personal or professional history? Your personality? Your value set? Your mindset? Define why this isn't a noteworthy fear for you.

CORE FEAR 3:
FEAR OF DISAPPOINTMENT

"The beauty is that through disappointment you can gain clarity, and with clarity comes conviction and true originality."

- CONAN O'BRIEN, COMEDIAN + TV HOST

In the Ideal Community chapter, we learned the importance of not pleasing everyone, and that repelling certain people is 100% necessary. If you struggle with people pleasing that section may have been a difficult one for you, and it may have tapped into your biggest fear, the Fear of Disappointment.

The Fear of Disappointment is a common fear that crushes us when you hear, "I'm disappointed in you," or you're afraid or assume you've made someone mad or offended them. Having an individual or a group of people disappointed in you can make you physically ill and wreck your emotional and mental state.

If you allow the Fear of Disappointment to hold you back from taking risks or stepping into your purpose, what kind of life is that?

Oprah Winfrey said, "You cannot live a brave life without disappointing some people, and the people who are rooting for your rise, will not be disappointed. The only people who will be disappointed are the people who have their own agenda."

Think about that. Think about the people who genuinely care about you and are rooting for you in life and in your career or business. They may be your family, friends, coworkers, mentors, or local community, and they want you to succeed. Focus your attention on them. Focus your attention on the people in the cheering section of your personal stadium, not the ones outside the gate circling like vultures. Focus on the ones who really matter and will be there through your ups and your downs.

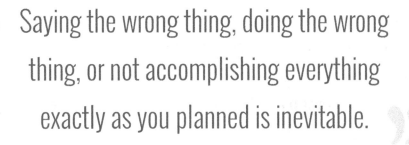

Saying the wrong thing, doing the wrong thing, or not accomplishing everything exactly as you planned is inevitable.

Saying the wrong thing, doing the wrong thing, or not accomplishing everything exactly as you planned is inevitable. So, when it happens, ask yourself, "How will my greatest supporters respond?" Will they uplift you and encourage you to try again and press on? Of course, they will.

The ones who genuinely love you will always support you, even when you fall flat on your face. The ones that don't support you and maliciously celebrate when you fail, are the vultures just waiting to pick at you and tell you "I told you so," when you fall. Those vultures must be confronted and distanced from your life immediately. They have not earned a space in your cheering section. Grab the big, bald, tatted-up bouncer at the door and have them kicked out.

The truth is, we are human and we make mistakes. Failure is inevitable. However, what makes you a seasoned and matured Connection-Based Leader is how you respond when those disappointments arise. How will you respond when you don't meet expectations? Will you respond with a defeatist perspective questioning, "Why should I even try anymore? I will just mess it up anyway!" Or will you lead with a progressive perspective of, "Yeah, that sucked. I really messed up, but now, I know what not to do. I know what mistakes I can grow from!"

It's your choice how you respond. Your response during difficult times tells your Community the kind of person and leader you are when things don't go your way. How you respond is a continuation of your Connection-Based Brand narrative. Show up with strength and vulnerability, show up with class, and show up as a leader who is ready to serve even when the times are rough. Be the example. Be the leader.

FEAR OF DISAPPOINTMENT: QUESTIONS

If the Fear of Disappointment is something you struggle with or want to dig deeper into, process and answer the following questions.

1. **Who are most afraid of disappointing?**

   Is it yourself? Your partner? Your kids? Your family? Your team? Your co-workers? Your employer? Random people? Who would you be devastated by if you disappointed them?

2. **What is the biggest thing you could do to disappoint others?**

   Think about your personal actions. Think about your professional projects and how you operate. What would be the worst thing you could do to disappoint others?

3. **When you disappoint others, how will you respond? What will you do?**

   Will you have a defeatist perspective or a progressive perspective, and why?

4. **When you disappoint others, what will they do?**

   How will they respond? Positively? Negatively? With understanding and grace? With hostility?

5. **If they respond negatively, do you think you should reevaluate that relationship?**

   What type of boundaries could you set?

6. **If they respond positively, what can you do to nurture that relationship?**

   If you have disappointed them and they still support you through it, what can you do to invest more time in building that healthy relationship?

7. **If you DON'T feel or experience the Fear of Disappointment, why do you think that is?**

   Think about why this fear doesn't strongly affect you. Is it your personal or professional history? Your personality? Your value set? Your mindset? Define why this isn't a noteworthy fear for you.

CORE FEAR 4:
FEAR OF INADEQUACY

"Our deepest fear is not that we are inadequate. Our deepest fear is that we are powerful beyond measure. It is our Light, not our Darkness, that most frightens us. And as we let our own light shine, we unconsciously give other people permission to do the same."

— MARIANNE WILLIAMSON, AUTHOR

It's midnight. I am in my writing cave (which is composed of me, my favorite chair with 4 blankets, my laptop and my Wonder Woman mug full of hot tea), and I am just about to write this section about the Fear of Inadequacy. However, I don't feel like the content and examples I have are adequate *(ha! go figure!)*.

I know this is one of the most common fears we all experience, so I want to do this topic justice. As the clock inches towards 1:00am, I decide to ask my Connection Crew Community on Instagram for their feedback on this topic.

I ask them if they've experienced the Fear of Inadequacy, and if they do, if they feel it more in their personal or professional life. I also ask them to share any specific stories or examples they have experienced with this fear.

After posting, I set my phone down and decide to go to bed.

In the morning, I woke up to hundreds of notifications!

It was clear this topic hit a nerve with our Community. Of everyone polled, 99% said that they felt the Fear of Inadequacy, and over 75% said it showed up mostly in their professional life. I also received countless messages saying that it showed up equally in both their professional and personal life.

When it was time to read everyone's stories, shit got real.

The stories the Connection Crew shared with me were personal, vulnerable, and real. Here are a few of the stories they shared:

"I feel the Fear of Inadequacy every day, that's why I am not getting paid for what I'm worth. I am letting fear determine my salary, not me."

"I feel inadequate every time I think about starting my own business, so it still hasn't happened yet."

"As soon as I wake up, I fear I won't be enough for those depending on me as a wife, mother and friend."

"I always feel like a fraud or something is wrong with me."

"I felt this fear during my cancer treatment. I wanted to advocate for my health and what I felt like my body was telling me, but would always default to what others wanted, since they were considered 'the experts.'"

"Working as a woman in a male dominated industry, I feel inadequate every day. I especially feel it when I need to take time off for family. The social pressure to be a good mom but also a good worker is crippling and exhausting."

I feel most inadequate when I think about the income inequality in my marriage. My husband earns more than me, so I feel like I have to make up for it in other ways."

"When I was brand new in my career, I was asked to take the lead to negotiate a $20 million-dollar construction contract with a large construction company. I would be facing off with the VP who was years into his career. Maybe it was the large, intimidating conference room or the fact that I lacked experience, but I was terrified."

"I feel most inadequate when I start comparing myself to my competitors."

"Every time I'm launching a new service, I believe no one will want it and my business will fail."

"I feel like an imposter, like, how did I con these people into hiring me?"

"I'm afraid to go after clients because it's not comfortable. I am afraid of being rejected and deemed not good enough."

"I'm a personal trainer, so feeling like I'm not fit enough to lead classes. Like I have to be the standard they should be reaching for, but I realize I am just projecting those expectations on myself. The reality is my clients like working with someone who is real and struggles alongside them."

"I feel inadequate when hiring people. Like who am I to make that call? Am I even qualified?"

"In my personal life, I am not good at small talk, and get anxiety about making plans so I often bail on people. I feel like I am a shitty friend. I feel like I don't have the makeup of what a good friend looks like."

"It feels like I need to prove myself and my worth at work. Even though I am told I am great, my own voice is telling me it's never enough."

Can you relate to any of those stories? the Fear of Inadequacy is clearly alive and well and making itself comfortable in our homes, at work, and in our minds.

It is much easier to downplay our great qualities, think less of ourselves, and believe that we are inadequate than it is to stand confident in who we are, and risk being perceived as cocky or arrogant. Society has taught us that appearing like we have it together is bad and means we are self-involved. And for most of us, the fear of being viewed as self-involved is way worse than feeling the Fear of Inadequacy.

Whenever you start to hear the Fear of Inadequacy start whispering in your ear, "Who are you to do this?" or "You are wasting everyone's time." or "You are charging too much." or "You aren't good enough," that is your cue to tell the Fear of Inadequacy to get to the back of the bus and say (yes, out loud), "Hey ...

> You're not welcome here!
> My Community needs to hear my voice.
> My Community needs to feel seen through my story.
> My Community needs to be served with my work.
> Yes, I am scared, but I am valuable and have to keep going.
> I am valuable and have to keep going.
> I am valuable and have to keep going.
> I AM VALUABLE AND HAVE TO KEEP GOING!
> AND YOU WILL NOT STOP ME!"

You are absolutely more than enough! You have tremendous value and something unique to share (remember your Gap?). This Inadequacy

Monster has made it their mission to deflate you and your confidence. This fear is powerful, but so are you. You are armed with your Connection-Based Brand to fight the Fear of Inadequacy. Use your Branding Words to remind you who you are and use your Ideal Community to remind you who you are fighting for and use your Gap to remind you that you have something unique and your place in line is rightfully yours.

FEAR OF INADEQUACY: QUESTIONS

If the Fear of Inadequacy is something you struggle with or want to dig deeper into, process and answer the questions below. The more you can define and understand this fear in your world, the more power you reclaim and the more your confidence is able to grow and flourish.

1. **When do you feel most inadequate?**

   When you take a new job? When you sign on a new client? Dealing with money? Family responsibilities? New opportunities? You don't look a certain way? You think others can do it better? Learning new systems? What opens the floodgates of inadequacy for you?

2. **What helps you fight the feelings of inadequacy?**

   Think about people, resources, books, or processes that motivate, affirm, and validate you. Be sure you are aware of what they are and have them on hand to fight the Fear of Inadequacy when it shows up.

3. **Who do you have in your life to fight the feelings of inadequacy?**

This is the key weapon to fight this fear, so make sure you define your "life raft" supporters who will affirm you. Friends, family, mentors, leaders, team members. Identify, by name, the people you can call on to rescue you when you are drowning in feelings of inadequacy.

4. **If you DON'T feel or experience the Fear of Inadequacy, why do you think that is?**

Think about why this fear doesn't strongly affect you. Is it your personal or professional history? Your personality? Your value set? Your mindset? Define why this isn't a noteworthy fear for you.

CORE FEAR 5:
FEAR OF THE UNKNOWN

"The oldest and strongest emotion of mankind is fear, and the oldest and strongest kind of fear is fear of the unknown."

-H.P. LOVECRAFT, AUTHOR

If the Five Core Fears were a pack of wolves, the Fear of the Unknown would be the alpha-dog, the pack leader, the biggest, baddest, most gnarly, seen-some-shit, and done-some-shit wolf of the group.

The Fear of the Unknown is who all the other Core Fears report back to. It's the general, it's the king on the fear throne.

The Fear of the Unknown is the source fear, the overarching fear, and the foundational fear that all other Core Fears are built upon. Just look at each of the other four Core Fears. You will see that each one of them can be traced back and linked to the Fear of the Unknown.

⇨ Fear of Others' Opinions: not knowing how others will respond—*Fear of the Unknown.*

⇨ Fear of Failure or Success: not knowing if your efforts will be worth it or what the expectations will be–*Fear of the Unknown.*

⇨ Fear of Disappointment: not knowing how your actions will affect others—*Fear of the Unknown.*

⇨ Fear of Inadequacy: not knowing if you are good enough—*Fear of the Unknown.*

The Fear of the Unknown rears it's ugly head because we lack a sense of control. We are overwhelmed because literally anything is possible and anything can happen. This is true both in experiencing a positive outcome and a painful one. Our intuition tells us to avoid potentially experiencing pain, so we focus our attention, energy, and mind on overthinking what could negatively happen. What could potentially cause us pain if we put ourselves out there, versus how it could positively affect our life.

The Fear of the Unknown can show up in the form of anxiety, overthinking, excessive worry, passivity, laziness, indecisiveness and assuming inaccurate, uninformed, or false information is true.

Even though the Fear of the Unknown is a beast and overall fear ringleader, we can use this to our advantage. Since there is only one leader, it provides a simple and tangible starting place for you to process fear.

Keep in mind that this is not an attempt to downplay your fear or the traumatic life events or deeply rooted insecurities where fear is tied to. No, this is an attempt to deconstruct fear. To make it not so big, overwhelming, and impossible to manage. This is an attempt to simplify fear so you can take the power back, so you're not hindered by its power when you decide to put yourself out there and share your Connection-Based Brand.

FEAR OF THE UNKNOWN: THE QUESTIONS

When you start to feel anxious or feel fear start bubbling up, I want you to process fear by asking two questions.

Question 1: As yourself, "Is this the Fear of the Unknown?"

If you say "yes," ask yourself the second question,

Question 2: "What am I afraid is going to happen?"
I am afraid of what people will say about me.
I am afraid of doing a horrible job.
I am afraid of letting everyone down.

I am afraid of not being experienced enough to take on this task.

Go back to the list of the Core Fears and identify which one(s) are tied to you fear thoughts and process through the questions for each fear. This process is to help show you that fear becomes manageable when it becomes tangible.

> " Fear becomes manageable
> when it becomes tangible. "

When you can identify and define what fear you are meeting, then you are equipped to lead it rather than it leading you as you step out and share your Connection-Based Brand.

DEFINE YOUR CORE FEARS: THE QUESTIONS

When we let our fears run wild in our head, it feels like there are so many, and it is impossible to tackle them all. However, if you take a step back and assess your specific fears, define them, and write them down, they become more manageable and not so paralyzing when they pop up.

Once you identify your Core Fear(s) it is simpler to attack one big thing vs a thousand little things. The following questions are here to help you dig even deeper into fear so you are empowered and ready to meet them head on in the real world.

The following questions are here to provide a personalized path to define your fears. Knowing what fears you consistently meet on the daily will help determine whether your Connection-Based Brand will be allowed to flourish, grow and make an impact, or if it will be immobilized and evaporated by fear. Fear will always be waiting for you as will success and impact, so let's define your fears so you can freely give your energy, mindset and emotional bandwidth to the positive outcomes and the success that is waiting for you.

As you work through the following questions, promise me one thing, be honest with yourself. There is no judgement here, my friend. This is the place for you—not for the masses. The more honest and vulnerable you are with your thoughts and your truths, the better!

Trigger Warning: The following questions are heavy. Be gentle with yourself and know you are not alone. Your fears have value, and you are not wrong or bad for having them. Take care as you go through them.

DIVE DEEPER QUESTIONS: EXPLORE YOUR FEAR

1. **Go look back at the Five Core Fears. Which Fear hit home?** Which fear do you feel shows up on the regular? What do you think are the 1-2 main fears that all your smaller fears link back to?

2. **What is the biggest fear or insecurity you have with expanding your business or career?**

   Think about what fear shows up when you are presented a new opportunity.

3. **What is something currently in your business that you are afraid to do?**

   It's time to get specific. Think about all the fears that have held you back from launching/growing a business or going after growth in your career. What is the fear you are choosing to use as a shield to protect yourself?

4. **What are your greatest fears?**

   What are your greatest fears in business? Greatest fears in life? Greatest fears in stepping out and growing your business and sharing your brand? What is the biggest thing you are afraid of that may be preventing you from taking the leap?

5. **Do you feel that being fearful is something you have turned into a habit?**

   Has turning to fear become an automatic, unconscious response for you?

6. **Realistically, what would happen if what you set out to do (no matter how small or big) didn't turn out as you expected?**

THE 5 CORE FEARS | 267

What would it look like if you failed? What would it look like if you "disappointed" people? What would actually happen? Realistically, what would people say if you failed? How would you be able to come back from this experience?

7. **Realistically, what would happen if you set out to do the thing(s) you were afraid of and it turned out well?**
   What would it look like if you succeeded? Realistically, what would people say if you succeeded?

8. **If you pushed past your fear, would you cause harm or cause good things for your Community?**
   Think about the Community outside of yourself. They are literally waiting for you to step out and serve them. If you pushed past fear and took action, would it positively add to their life?

9. **Have you given yourself permission to succeed?**
   Why or why not?

THE 5 CORE FEARS
Wrap Up

I know, this was a monstrous chapter. Thank you for trusting me to open the fear floodgates, and for being completely honest with yourself. Fear is something we don't talk about enough, let alone in a branding book. However, this section is a key part to *The Connection Method* to help you define the fears you will meet once you step out and share your Connection-Based Brand.

Understanding your Core Fear(s) will help you recognize them when they show up, so you are able to acknowledge them, process them, and keep going, instead of letting them hold you hostage.

Fear is the only thing stopping you from moving forward in life and in business. Being able to define your fear, change your perception of how you process fear is a powerful and actionable item that gives you freedom from the talons of fear. It empowers you, validates you and gives you permission to show up as you in your Connection-Based Brand.

Defining your fear allows you to be a real, relatable and an impactful Connection-Based Leader who can connect with their Ideal Community by pushing through the reality of fear. When you can do that, you are provided yet another opportunity for your Community to feel seen, feel heard and know that they matter, not only through your Connection-Based Brand message, but also through the story of your grit and perseverance.

As we close not only this chapter on fear, but also *The Connection Method* section, I want you to take time and reflect on the journey you just went on. You dug deep, you worked hard and created something you can be proud of taking out and sharing with your Community.

You are about to take a giant leap. You are about to step out from hiding behind the safety of the "it's not personal, it's business" mindset and the "perfect logo and business card" branding mentality and are ready to step out and show *you*. You are stepping out and sharing your Connection-Based Brand. You have answered all the questions, you have done all the work. Now it's time to stop asking and start acting.

THE FIVE CORE FEARS

In this chapter you learned:

⇨ That fear will be waiting for you as you step out and share your Connection-Based Brand.

⇨ That defining your fear will give you power to understand your fear and manage your fear to allow your Connection-Based Brand to grow.

⇨ That there are Five Core Fears:

5 core fears {

CORE FEAR *1.* Fear of Others' Opinions

CORE FEAR *2.* Fear of Failure or Success

CORE FEAR *3.* Fear of Disappointment

CORE FEAR *4.* Fear of Inadequacy

CORE FEAR *5.* Fear of The Unknown

⇨ The questions to help you identify your fear and make it tangible.

⇨ The Core Fear(s) you directly experience.

⇨ That you are a badass and won't let fear hold you back!

PART 3
Using Your Brand

CHAPTER ELEVEN

THE 5 DECIDING QUESTIONS

"Your overwhelm is due to a lack of decision making.

- JERESHIA HAWK, BUSINESS COACH

POP THE BUBBLY!!! THROW THE CONFETTI!!!! YOU DID IT!!!!!! You have worked so hard in the previous chapters, you have now defined your very own, unique to you, Connection-Based Brand! Wahoo! You're a total badass and you should be so proud of yourself! I know I am! I'm beaming! I'm so excited for you, and I'm the proudest Branding Mama!

This is a big moment, so, just like if you were heading to your high school prom, I want you to pose for a picture because this moment needs to be remembered.

Fix your dress or tweak your tux and stand on the bottom of the stairs with your date, your Connection-Based Brand. I want to capture this moment forever before you two head out the door and go out into the world!

Click!

Click! Click!

Damn, you two look good!

As you stand there on the stairs posing for 1,001 more pictures, and rolling your eyes because your Branding Mama is embarrassing you, you are excited about walking out the door, but you also feel prickles of anxiety start to creep into your body.

You start to wonder, "Yeah this is all so exciting, but what now? What am I supposed to do with my date, my Connection-Based Brand? Am I even ready to go out with them? Will they actually be there for me as I awkwardly step out into the real world?"

Feeling nervous, anxious, excited and a little bit awkward is absolutely normal and expected at this stage of building and sharing your Connection-Based Brand.

In these final chapters we will go over how to actually *use* your Connection-Based Brand. From how to make decisions to marketing yourself and your brand, you will be equipped with the tools to know exactly how to deliver your Connection-Based Brand message. You will learn how to use it as a tool to give you clarity and self-validate yourself in times of overthinking and overwhelm, and above all, give you a resource to stay consistent and be confident in who you are and what you offer!

YOUR BRANDING BATTLE BAG

I once dated a guy who was one of six children, which, as you can imagine, made his mother an actual, living saint. She was a no-nonsense and ready-for-anything woman, and she fittingly had a large purse the size of Texas which, without fail, went with her everywhere she went.

The entire family referred to this bag as her Battle Bag, and for good reason. Having six children and countless grandchildren, she had everything she needed to tend to a scraped knee, feeding a hangry grandchild, or to surviving a full-on zombie apocalypse in that bag.

I am sure that some of you out there are familiar with this type of bag, and many of you might even own one yourself. It's a bag that makes you prepared and ready for anything!

In the previous chapters, you assembled your very own Branding Battle Bag.

Through each section, you added branding elements that you can whip out of your bag when you need to stay consistent, implement your brand, give you permission to be yourself, make decisions, validate yourself, define and push past fear, or perhaps even survive a zombie apocalypse (after all, your Connection-Based Brand is immensely powerful!).

Currently in your Branding Battle Bag are your defined branding elements: your Branding Words, your Ideal Community Attract + Repel Lists, your Gap, your Niche, your Value Proposition, and your Core Fear(s).

Individually, these branding elements are powerful tools, but together they are a nuclear force of validation, decisive power, consistency, confidence, and clarity.

Your Brand Battle Bag is a powerful weapon against overthinking and self-doubt. It is your tool kit to help direct you, help get you out of your own way, validate you, and help you to make confident decisions so you can move forward and progress in both life and business!

MAKING DECISIONS

Being able to make confident decisions as an entrepreneur, business owner or leader is the only way you can move forward and grow. Most of us stay stuck in our own heads, overthinking all the options when a circumstance, opportunity or decision presents itself or we get stuck in the self-doubt or second-guessing brain tornado wondering what to choose or if we made the right choice.

Non-stop mind chatter like, "What should I post on social media?"

"Should I take on this new client?"

"What will people say if I ...?"

"Should I take on this new project?"

"Which option should I choose?"

"Did I make the right choice?"

"Did I say the right things?"

This mind chatter is exhausting and runs rampant like an over caffeinated, twitchy squirrel. Unless you have a clear strategy to make confident decisions, that twitchy squirrel will have free rein of your mind.

Which, we know is not a healthy way to live or operate your business, or lead your Community in any capacity.

So that's where your Branding Battle Bag comes in. You now have a bag full of clearly defined branding elements, that provide a filter and direction so you can make decisions with confidence and most importantly, with intentionality.

Yes, intentionality. Intentionality is key.

When you lead with intentionality, you will know *why* you should or shouldn't do something. Leading with intentionality provides you with the kind of decisive power you need to stay consistent and confident with who you are and what you offer.

I know I refer to my queen, Oprah Winfrey, a lot in this book, but for good reason. No one knows more about the power of intentionality than her. In 2014, Oprah was interviewed by a room of Stanford business graduate students, where she shared the secret to why her show was the number one talk show for 25 years straight. She said, "I told my producers, do not bring me a show unless you have fully thought out what is your intention for doing it. I don't do anything without being fully clear about why I intend to do it. The intention is going to determine the action or result or consequence."

If being intentional with her decisions and actions is the driving force behind one of the world's most powerful, successful, impactful, and influential individuals in history, then I think it is something we should pay attention to and integrate, don't you agree?

The definition of intention is done on purpose, or deliberate.

That's where your branding elements in your Branding Battle Bag in combination with the 5 Deciding Questions will come into play to help you make deliberate decisions, choices and moves with purpose.

The 5 Deciding Questions are five powerful questions that that you must ask yourself every time you make a decision, second guess yourself, are confused, unconfident, or the twitchy thought squirrel is running circles in your in your head.

These 5 Deciding Questions are your extremely discerning best friend who guides you in the right direction and gives you the straight up answer you need.

As you go through these questions, think about a current circumstance, a pending decision, or a scenario that is happening in your life or business right now. It can be as small as, "Should I include this specific client testimonial on my website?" or "What should I wear on a photoshoot?" Or bigger questions such as, "Should I invest in developing a whole new product line for my business?" or "Should I switch careers?" or "Should I say yes to this gigantic new opportunity?"

No matter the question, decision, opportunity, circumstance, or idea you have in front of you, your first response should always be to ask yourself these 5 Deciding Questions.

Please have your defined branding elements (Branding Words, Ideal Community Attract/Repel Lists, Gap, Niche and Value Proposition) on hand as you go through the following questions.

THE FIVE DECIDING QUESTIONS

QUESTION 1

Does this opportunity, circumstance or thought coordinate with, encourage, promote and/or align with my Branding Words?

This is the number one question for a reason, because if you answer "no" to it, then you can stop here, you have your answer—it's a no, a hard pass!

However, if you say "yes" to this answer, then you can move onto question number 2!

Remember, your Branding Words are the first filter every decision, thought or opportunity needs runs through. They provide the path for consistency and clarity, so let them help you. Let them guide you. That's what they're here to do!

For years, I have run both my life and business, and make intentional decisions based on just this one question. For me, no matter how big or small a decision, if an opportunity does not provide a way for me to be real, educational, empowering, inspirational and share my joy, then why would I accept it?

Even if I have all the "but, it's ..." or the "but, it would be ..." excuses and justifications in the world, if it does not align with my Branding Words, which are the heart of my brand, my business, and myself, then the answer is a clear no—even if it's uncomfortable or might disappoint others.

If the answer to this question is no, then you have two options.

The first option is to graciously decline the opportunity and then confidently move on, knowing why you made the right decision, because it didn't align with your values and brand standards. Saying "no" gives you the time and availability for opportunities that do align with your Branding Words. Saying no to inconsistency, opens up possibilities for "yes" opportunities. Staying no to inconsistency, is the best way to serve and respect your Community.

A second option if you answer is no, is to change the circumstances, so it does align with your Branding Words. If you can't do this, or it's not worth your time, then slap a big "No thank you, I'll pass" sticker on it, and move your cute buns down the road. There is something bigger and better waiting for you. I promise.

Your Branding Words are your first stop in the decision-making process and will help transition your mind from excuses, justification, and self-doubt to something tangible that you can evaluate from a logical, strategic, and more centered place.

Always start with your Branding Words. They are your trusty compass when you feel lost.

QUESTION 2

Does this opportunity, circumstance or thought attract my Ideal Community? Will it attract the kind of people that will energize, excite, and uplift me?

I would say that this question is as equally important as the first, and in my experience, provides the most clarity in the shortest amount of time. It's a biggie, so I want you to memorize it, and have it at the ready whenever you need to make ANY decision, or you find yourself starting to second guess yourself for any reason.

The first thing you need to do is whip out your Ideal Community Attract and Repel lists from your Branding Battle Bag and remind both your brain and heart exactly the type of person you want to attract and repel. It's time to shuffle those excuses to the side and bring your focus back to who you committed to attract and serve—your Attract List.

Visualize the outcome and think about if you said yes. Would saying yes open doors to attract people on your Attract List, or will it open the door to attract people from your Repel List?

If it doesn't attract your Ideal Community, then why would you invest your time, energy, and resources into supporting it? If you say "yes" to something that attracts individuals from your Repel List, then you are literally turning your back on your Attract List Ideal Community and saying, "No, I don't want to work with you."

You set the narrative for who you work with, so make sure whatever you do is consistent with your Attract List.

QUESTION 3

Does this opportunity cater to, serve, or provide value to those in my Ideal Community who are searching for solutions in my specific Niche?

Just like in the previous two questions, you need to put your opportunity, circumstance, or thought through the Branding Element filter of your defined Niche.

Remember, the goal is to be consistent and focused on your specific offering. You must be intentional with your decisions and actions, so you can build depth in one area.

You need to make sure that you are spending your precious time and talents on things that support and provide value within your specific Niche. Avoid stepping outside of your lane and confusing your Community by offering something outside of your specialty and spreading yourself too thin.

As you ask yourself the Niche question, remember, your Ideal Community is more connected and confident about a brand that is consistent and that they know what to expect. *They* need you to say no to things that divert from what you specialize in. They need you to:

⇨ Stay in your lane and become their personal expert in that space.

⇨ Make it easy for them to know how to explain to their friends who you are.

⇨ Make it clear how you serve them.

Now, with this being said, if you are new to your industry and are still exploring where to concentrate your efforts, or you have a reached a point in your career where you need to expand and grow, you absolutely should feel free to explore and try new things. Your Niche is able to grow and flex with you. However, if you do, check in, and ensure that it aligns with your Branding Words, Ideal Community, and overall branding mission.

QUESTION 4

If I say yes to this opportunity, will I feel good promoting it and sharing that I am involved with it?

I've shared this question with my clients and the general response is, "Oh shit! I've never thought about that!"

Most of the time we stay in our own head, looking only at ourselves, and forget to evaluate the overall, greater perception, and energy around the opportunity, circumstance, or thought in question.

If you are faced with the opportunity to be involved with a group of people, a new company, a new position, an event, or activity, consider the overall vibe and mission they have. Would you feel confident attaching your brand, your name, and your reputation to it and promoting it?

Step outside of yourself and remember you define the narrative of your brand, especially when expanding out and associating with others. You have to check to make sure that they share the same values as you do in order for it to be a beneficial opportunity for both of you.

Think about who you would be working with. What is their mission, agenda, values or focus? What type of perception does this opportunity, circumstance or thought already have associated with them? Look at the big picture of how an opportunity is perceived by the larger Community and how you would feel being connected to it?

If you feel excited and confident, your values are aligned and everything remains consistent with the previous three questions, then rock on and go for it! But if there is a little voice telling you something is off or things aren't matching up with the first three questions, then you need to change the circumstance or to pass all together.

QUESTION 5

If I say no to this opportunity, how will I feel? If I say yes to the opportunity, how will I feel?

If you've made it to this final question and are still on the fence with what to do, this question should help you make the final decision which direction you should go.

 This question comes with stipulations though. You *must* be completely honest with yourself, and allow the most truthful answers to come through, even if you don't like them. This is the time to focus on throwing out your inner people pleaser, and focus on what's best for *y-o-u*.

Listen to your gut, your instincts, and your intuition. Address the butterflies in your stomach. Are the butterflies dancing with joy because you are nervous-excited about stepping into something new that aligns perfectly with your Connection-Based Brand? Or are those butterflies flapping their wings in Morse Code telling you to run, run far far away from this scenario?

If you are still on the fence or suffer from being a people pleaser, consider this: if disappointing people or the fear of people not liking you was off the table, and all you had to worry about was what was best for you, your brand and business, what direction would you go?

I can't tell you how many times I answered the "if I say no" question with "I would feel relieved, at peace, and free!" If you have this response, this answer is generally a red flag and telling you exactly what decision you need to make.

> " Listen to your gut, your instincts are there to help you, not hurt you. "

The branding elements in your Branding Battle Bag are there to provide a pathway to clarity, however, your instincts are the most powerful tool you have. Listen to your gut, your instincts are there to help you, not hurt you.

THE 5 DECIDING QUESTIONS

Does this opportunity, circumstance or thought coordinate, encourage, promote and/or align with my Branding Words?

Does this opportunity, circumstance or thought attract my Ideal Community? Will it attract the kind of people that will energize, excite, and uplift me?

Does this opportunity cater to, serve, or provide value to those in my Ideal Community who are searching for solutions in my specific Niche?

If I say yes to this opportunity, circumstance or thought, will I feel good about promoting it and sharing that I was involved with it?

If I DON'T say yes to this opportunity, circumstance or thought, how will I feel? If I DO say yes, how will I feel?

THE FIVE DECIDING QUESTIONS:
Wrap Up

I know how it is. The twitchy squirrel in your brain likes to take over, and making decisions is sometimes not that simple. Even after going through The Five Deciding Questions, we tend to *choose* to keep overthinking or *choose* to hold onto self-doubt.

> " We tend to choose to keep overthinking or choose to hold onto self-doubt. "

We *allow* the justifications and the ifs, ands, or buts excuses to hold us back from moving forward and making the decisions we need to make—big or small. We all reach a point where we resist and don't want to accept the reality of a decision, but in the end, it's a choice.

Overthinking is uncomfortably comfortable.

When we finally make a decision, it means we have to take action, which is not comfortable. When we finally make a decision, it means we can no longer sit there in thought, but it's time to take the leap. Making decisions pushes us out of our comfort zone, which is a necessary step to push us also towards growth.

These questions help you get out of your own way and are the jet fuel you need to push yourself to decide and take action in a circumstance you've been holding onto for too long.

If something is not going to be a positive resource or opportunity in your life, it has no business being in your business. Say no and let it go. Plain and simple. No justification. No overthinking. No self-doubt. No mind games. None of that. The discussion has ended. You have your answer.

THE 5 DECIDING QUESITONS

In this chapter you learned:

⇨ About your Branding Battle Bag. This bag is full of your branding elements (Branding Words, Ideal Community, etc.) to help you navigate overthinking and help you make decisions.

⇨ The 5 Deciding Questions to help you navigate both large and small opportunities and decisions that come your way.

CHAPTER TWELVE

BRANDING VS MARKETING

*"Branding is your message. Marketing is how that message
is delivered."*

- THE CONNECTION METHOD

At the beginning of this book, I shared the two common misconceptions people have about branding. The first, that branding is merely visuals, like our logo and colors. The second, is that branding is the same as social media or marketing. After going through *The Connection Method*, you now know that it's way more than either of these two!

Branding and marketing are two separate concepts but work together as partners. Now that you have a solid definition of your Connection-Based

Brand, we can dive into the difference between branding and marketing and how to deliver an effective and Connection-Based Marketing strategy.

When I start discussing the topic of marketing, everyone seems to collectively perk up to hear my secret strategies behind successful marketing and leveraging social media. Sorry Crew, that's not what we are going to dive into today. I am first and foremost your Branding Mama, not your source for hot social media tips and tricks.

With the rapid change of technology, by the time this book is published, any marketing or social media suggestions I give would be old news. So, my intention for this section is to give you a broad view of the relationship between branding and marketing and how you can market the message of your Connection-Based Brand using an approach that is relevant for delivering your message today, tomorrow, and decades from now.

Whether you are an entrepreneur, business owner or leader in an organization, delivering intentional marketing is the final piece to help you step out with your Connection-Based Brand. If you are a business owner, you will use marketing to share and promote your product and service directly to your Community. If you are a leader within an organization, you will use marketing to share and promote the unique skill set you have to offer like on your resume, interviewing for a promotion or proposing a new project. Whether you are marketing your business or marketing yourself as a leader, learning how to share your message with Connection-Based Marketing will be key in helping you stand out and level up.

WHAT'S THE DIFFERENCE?

Your Connection-Based Brand is the foundation from which everything else will evolve, filter through, and give you clarity and consistency as you navigate your business or leadership role. Your brand is your *message*. Your message is something you've personally curated, something you are grounded in, something that is concrete and consistent.

This message you have created has to get out into the world somehow, and that is where marketing comes in. Marketing is how your message is *delivered*. It is the vessel in which your message can be transported from point A to point B and distributed to your Community.

> Your brand is your message.
> Marketing is how your message is delivered.

Think about the relationship between branding and marketing as train tracks and a train car. Branding is the train tracks and marketing is the train car.

Branding train tracks provide guidance between point A (you/your brand) and point B (your Community). They are foundational, concrete and are anchored to the ground. Your tracks keep the route consistent and aligned, tethering you back to your values and who you are.

Marketing is the train car. The train car is the vessel where you pour your branding message into and then how it's delivered to your Community.

Your train car contains various messages that are anchored to your brand tracks. If you ever feel scattered with your marketing, chances are, you have allowed your marketing train car to get derailed from your brand train tracks and is flying down a hill with no guidance, no direction, and headed towards a dastardly end.

When starting out, most people forget about building their branding tracks first and pour their attention into the fun and alluring marketing. However, after the romance of marketing passes, and their marketing isn't yielding any return, they realize that they are riding on a runaway train car. They have built the train car before the tracks.

That's why it's so vital to start your marketing strategy by *first* defining your brand (which you've done, wahoo!). That way you can be intentional with your marketing, know what to say, how to say it and where to send your marketing train car.

CONNECTION-BASED MARKETING CYCLE

Having a clearly defined brand message and an intentional marketing strategy is vital, but there is one more element that comes into play in order to create an impactful Connection-Based Marketing strategy. Imagery.

Before you launch any kind of marketing campaign, you need to create intentional imagery to represent and illustrate your Connection-Based Brand.

The first step is to define your brand message (which you just did! Check!), the second step is to illustrate your message with custom imagery, and then the third step is to deliver that message and imagery via your marketing. This cycle provides you a path for consistency and connection as you share your Connection-Based Brand with your Community.

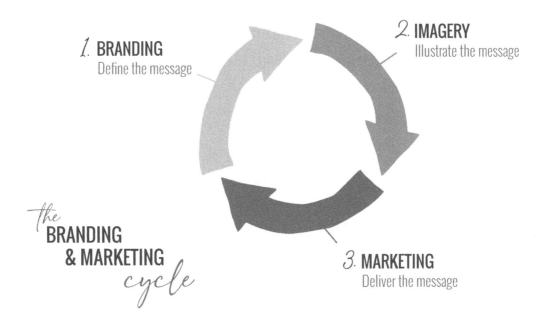

1. BRANDING
Define the message

2. IMAGERY
Illustrate the message

3. MARKETING
Deliver the message

the BRANDING & MARKETING *cycle*

Step 1: Define your brand message so you can move forward with consistency, direction, and intentionality with everything you do with imagery and how you deliver your message with marketing. This first step tells you what message to illustrate and deliver.

Step 2: Illustrate that message with custom imagery. Just say no to purely relying on stock photos, but instead, allow your Community to connect with you and your Connection-Based Brand via custom branding images that show you, your team, and your Community. These images can be from a professional photographer or even from your cell phone, the key is to show the person, people and process of your brand.

Step 3: Deliver your message via your marketing platform (website, social media, etc.). This is where you release and share your message and imagery, market your Connection-Based Brand and, in turn, open the door for connection with your Community.

> The cycle is a continual process. When it is time to create another marketing plan, strategy or post, the cycle starts over again.

The cycle is a continual process. When it is time to create another marketing plan, strategy or post, the cycle starts over again. Go back to your brand message, make sure the imagery and copy is consistent with your brand message, illustrate it, and then deliver your message. Repeat the cycle so you ensure your message is consistent to build the highest level of trust and confidence for both you and your Community.

BRANDING VS. MARKETING
Wrap Up

In order to effectively market your brand, you must first understand the role branding and marketing have with each other. After going through *The Connection Method*, you have a solid Connection-Based Brand that you can use to create marketing content that is intentional and consistent. When your brand leads your marketing, you will feel more streamlined and consistent versus feeling like you are throwing spaghetti at the wall to see what sticks.

Lead with your brand message, and then create custom imagery to illustrate that message. In the next chapter we will dig into how to create imagery that illustrates the heart of your brand and provides a way to deeply connect with your Community.

BRANDING VS. MARKETING

In this chapter you learned:

➪ **The difference between branding and marketing.**

- Branding is your message.

- Marketing is how that message is delivered.

➪ **About the Connection-Based Marketing cycle. This cycle is intended to keep you consistent and maximize connection and confidence with your Community.**

CHAPTER THIRTEEN

ILLUSTRATE YOUR MESSAGE

"Taking an image, freezing a moment, reveals how rich reality truly is."

- UNKNOWN

I have been a professional photographer for over a decade, and I specialize in Lifestyle Branding photography, a type of photography that goes beyond the headshot and illustrates the heart of you and your brand. Since this is my background, there was no way I was handing you a book without a little somethin' somethin' about how to create the most intentional images to illustrate your brand and be confident in front of the camera!

Keep in mind that you don't *only* need to use professional photos to illustrate your brand. For your website, yes, you need a library of custom, professional images to fill the pages of your site. However, for social media, it can absolutely be a mix of professional and casual photos taken from your phone.

Whether it's a professional image or a casual snapshot, your images need to be intentional. Your images need to have purpose and align with your brand. Create and use imagery that is consistent with your Branding Words and that attract your Ideal Community.

Your Community wants to know what to expect, they need you to calm their fear of the unknown, they want to see real. You must show them imagery that illustrates what you are all about.

This type of photography is called *branding photography*.

Before we dive in, I want to make clear the difference between the two types of branding photography: Personal Branding photography and Lifestyle Branding photography.

Personal Branding photography simply illustrates the person(s) behind the brand. It's a creative take on headshots. Most of the time these photos are done in a studio and are straight forward images of the person behind the business.

Lifestyle Branding on the other hand, is a more involved type of photography genre. Yes, it includes elements of personal branding photography, but it goes beyond that. Lifestyle Branding illustrates the real lifestyle of the person or people behind the business andbrand. Lifestyle Branding captures images of what it looks like to work with you, shares your personality and illustrates who you are in both the professional and personal world. The purpose of Lifestyle Branding photography is to create in-depth connection pieces between you and your Community via intentional, on brand, story-focused imagery.

> " The purpose of Lifestyle Branding photography is to create in-depth connection pieces between you and your Community via intentional, on brand, story-focused imagery. "

For example, I worked with a client whose Connection-Based Brand revolved around balancing being a mom and a business owner. While we captured the standard photos of her working on her computer and on her phone, we also captured images of her working alongside her 2-year-old daughter (who wore a "mini boss lady" t-shirt. Adorable). Additionally, we also captured images of the two reading books together in her daughter's playroom and taking a walk with the stroller.

When we finished with the photoshoot, my client looked at me and said, "I get it now. What we are capturing photos that literally represent my lifestyle. This is who I am, what I do for work and how I spend time with my daughter—this is me!"

Exactly. Lifestyle Branding images serve as visual connection pieces for your Community to see themselves in you, in your brand. These images are not about being showy and saying, "Look at me! Look how great I am!" They are about giving your Community the chance to say, "She's like me! I'm not alone." "I do the same thing he does!", "They are so my people!" Lifestyle Branding Photography provides the simplest and most direct path for others to feel seen, feel heard and know they matter.

That's the power of illustrating your Connection-Based Brand with Lifestyle Branding photography.

PHOTOSHOOT BASICS

Let's get to the brass tacks of a Lifestyle Branding photoshoot.

Here is the truth, it doesn't matter if you are working with a professional photographer, using your cell phone, taking photos with a self-timer, or running around town on a photo-safari adventure with a friend, you need to make sure you are intentional about the following five elements when you are in the planning process and during the photoshoot. These five elements are location, branding colors, wardrobe, posing, and your photographer.

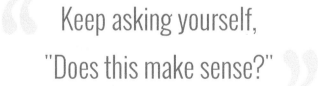

Keep asking yourself,
"Does this make sense?"

As you plan your photoshoot, be sure to have your Branding Words and Ideal Community Attract List on hand as you run through all five elements. When making decisions on how to illustrate your brand message, keep asking yourself, "Does this make sense?"

LOCATION

Location sets the tone for the story you are telling. If you are the star of the photoshoot, your location is the supporting role. What would *Sex and the City* be without New York City as the backdrop? What would *Harry Potter* be without Hogwarts? What would *Star Wars* be without "... a galaxy far, far away?" Your location sets the subconscious tone for your photos.

When choosing locations, find locations that make sense to you. Not ones that you should do because everyone else does, but because they make sense to you and your story, your brand.

If every morning you wake up and go read in a nook in your house with your favorite a cup of coffee, then your reading nook and mug of coffee need to be photographed.

If one of your core values and favorite things to do is spending time with family cooking in the kitchen, then do a photoshoot set with your family in the kitchen.

If hiking and outdoor activities are a big part of your lifestyle, then hit the trail with your photographer.

It doesn't matter what industry you are in; the point is, to illustrate your lifestyle in and outside of business. Your goal is to create those connection pieces where your Community can tangibly see themselves and connect.

BRANDING COLORS

When I work with my clients, next to defining their Branding Words, this is their second most anticipated conversation! It's important (as I have said time and time again) to define your Branding Words and overall brand message *before* you decide on the specific visuals of your brand such as your Branding Colors. That way, when you go through the list of colors and their meanings, you know exactly what colors to pick and why you are picking them because they align with your branding elements. So, make sure you have them on hand as you go through this next section!

> " The branding colors you choose will set the visual and subconscious tone for expressing your brand. "

The branding colors you choose will set the visual and subconscious tone for expressing your brand. They dictate what you wear, the graphics you choose, the tone of your website and online presence, and if implemented successfully, create a subconscious link between you and those colors.

When your Community is on social media or out and about, and they see your color(s), they will think of you because you have created a link between you and those colors. Branding Colors are an incredible way to keep you and your Connection-Based Brand on the forefront of people's minds.

In the following section, I will give you three steps for how to find and define your Branding Colors. I will also give you meanings of core primary colors and a few popular shades so you can find the best colors that illustrate and communicate your Connection-Based Brand.

STEP 1: LOOK FOR YOUR BRANDING COLOR

There is one spot in your house which holds the key to starting the process of defining your Branding Colors, and that spot is your closet.

Look at the items in your closet. What colors do you have a lot of, or naturally gravitate to? Is it blue and white? Pinks and yellows? Green and brown? Black and white? Remember, your brand shouldn't require a lot of maintenance, so it needs to start from where you already subconsciously sit with color.

If all you see is black in your closet, welcome to the club. This circumstance is quite common, and I call it, *The Black Factor*. Black is a powerful Branding Color, but it *might* not be the best color to represent you and your brand. If you fall prey to the Black Factor, think about other colors you gravitate to inspire you or spark connection.

Branding Colors have a way of calling to us before we even realize it. Listen to your intuition, look around at the colors around you, colors that inspire you or spark excitement and use those to move forward.

Once you have identified two to four colors, head to step 2.

If you have no idea where to begin with colors or are experiencing The Black Factor, move ahead to step 2 anyway. Read through the color meanings to see what aligns with your Branding Words and overall perception you wish to portray.

STEP 2: DEFINE YOUR BRANDING COLORS

The next step is to take your colors from step 1 and run them through the meanings of each color.

Do the meaning of the colors you identified match the tone and intention of your Branding Words? Will it attract and connect with your Ideal Community?

Keep in mind that your Branding Words don't necessarily have to match each specific word of a color meaning, but instead the overall essence of the color or shade.

> Make sure you are choosing colors out of intentionality, not your comfort zone.

Make sure you are choosing colors out of intentionality, not your comfort zone. Is your brand happy and upbeat? Then maybe yellow or orange might be a good fit. Is your brand powerful and luxurious? Then maybe gold or red could be your color. Is your brand clean and simple? Then perhaps white or beige could represent you well. Choose colors that align with your branding elements, your personality, overall aesthetic and essence you wish to portray.

If the colors you brought in from step 1 don't match your brand, then go through the color meanings and find colors that do align with your Branding Words and then commit to them!

BRANDING COLORS: WHAT THEY MEAN

BEIGE: Neutral, Calm, Relaxing, Dependable, Comfort.

BLACK: Formal, Dramatic,Excellence, Sophistication, Security, Power, Elegance, High End.

BLUE: Trust, Peace, Loyalty, Competence, Wisdom, Intelligence, Depth, Stability.

BROWN: Rugged, Dependable, Trustworthy, Simple, Grounded.

BURGUNDY: Sophistication, Luxury, High End, Power, Ambition. A shade of red.

CORAL: Warmth, Acceptance, Outgoing, Dynamic. A perfect combination of pink and orange.

GOLD: Opulence, Luxury, Extravagance, Wealth, Status, Abundance.

GREEN: Nature, Freshness, Growth, Harmony, Health, Healing, Quality.

GREY: Neutrality, Indifference, Conservative, Reserve, Grounded, Foundational, Solid.

HOT PINK: Rebel, Assertive, Energy, Attention. A shade of pink.

MAROON: Confidence, Ambition, Creativity, Risk, Excitement. A shade of purple.

MAUVE: Devotion, Renewal, Youth, Purity, Idealistic, Romantic. A shade of purple.

MINT: Refreshing, Inviting, Tranquil, Innocence. A shade of green.

NAVY: Power, Authority, Serious, Truth, Stable, Traditional. A shade of blue.

ORANGE: Enthusiasm, Success, Creativity, Adventure, Confidence, Bravery, Social, Warmth, Fun.

PINK: Compassion, Sincerity, Friendship, Sweet, Approachable, Sophistication, Playful.

PURPLE: Balance, Spirituality, Dignity, Wisdom, Independence, Ambition, Opulence, Luxury, Royal.

RED: Excitement, Love, Energy, Strength, Passion, Danger, Power, Sexy, Spicy.

SILVER: Sleek, Modern, Glamorous, Elegant, Sophisticated, High Tech.

TEAL: Commitment, Trust, Balance, Protection, Rational, Practical. A perfect blend of blue and green—an elevated version of Turquoise.

TURQUOISE: Calm, Growth, Energy, Uplifting. A perfect blend of blue and green.

WHITE: Clean, Simple, Honest, Sincere, Brilliance, Illumination.

YELLOW: Creativity, Happiness, Positivity, Warmth, Cheer, Joy, Positive, Enthusiasm.

What colors speak to you? What colors align with your Branding Words? What colors would attract your Ideal Community? If a certain color shade is not on the list, feel free to ask Google for help in learning the meaning.

Once you have gone through the color meanings and chose the colors that align and are consistent with your Connection-Based Brand, then, guess what? You have found your Branding Colors! Wahoo! Head to step 3 and own those colors!

STEP 3: OWN YOUR COLORS

The next step is to own your colors! Attach your brand to these colors. Wear them, use them, and integrate them into all aspect what you do! These are *your* colors, so share them with pride!

Commit to those colors even if they are out of your comfort zone or challenge you (especially if you've fallen prey to The Black Factor). Your Branding Colors are a subconscious way for your Community to understand who you are and a way to keep you on top of mind, so chose colors out of intentionality, not your comfort zone.

Once you own your Branding Colors, they will provide yet another way to feel confident and validate your actions through consistency.

BRANDING COLOR TROUBLESHOOTING:

TOO MANY COLORS

If you are someone who loves color and find yourself with too many colors to choose from, I recommend picking no more than three core colors that strongly convey your branding message. Sure, you can make a case for any color to be a part of your brand but stick with strongest options, what makes the most sense and the colors represents your brand well. Stick to no more than three core colors which represent you and visually communicate your Connection-Based Brand's mission. Keep in mind that in addition to these three colors, you can also have supportive colors like black, white or grey that act as complimentary colors when you start to create your brand visuals.

If you find that you still can't narrow down your color selection, then maybe the rainbow pattern is your Branding Color! If your brand is energetic, positive, inclusive and exudes joy and happiness, then it might be a great fit! You can learn more about Branding Color patterns in the next troubleshooting tip!

PRINTS CAN BE "COLORS"

Animal prints, camo, polka dot, rainbow, oh my! Yes, prints can be a Branding "Color!" If adding a specific print to your branding visuals accents your core Branding Colors and advances your overall Connection-Based Branding message, then go for it! Patterns are a great way to get even more specific with your brand visuals and another way to express your brand using prints in your wardrobe!

Here are a few common prints and their meanings:

Camo: Rugged, Conservative, Subdue. Tied to the military, combat, and hunting.

Checkered: Retro, Warm, Confident.

Chevron: Funky, Retro, Timeless.

Floral: Beautiful, Feminine, Nurturing.

Leopard or Cheetah Confident, Quick Wit, Sassy.

Polka Dot: Cheerful, Light, Retro, Energetic.

Rainbow: Happy, Joyful, Positive, Inclusive. Tied to the LGBTQ+ community.

Zebra Print: Balance, Yin/Yang, Wisdom.

As always, before you commit to a print, make sure that the print meanings align with your overall brand message and your Branding Words.

Secondly, make sure that whatever color you choose for your print stays consistent with your overall Branding Colors. For example, if you want to use cheetah print, make sure that the color you choose to share that print, such as brown, beige and black, are a part of your core Branding Colors.

WARDROBE: COLORS

Now that you have locked down your Branding Colors, it's time to let those colors guide you with how you present yourself in public, online and what to wear for photoshoots. Wardrobe is always the biggest question and source of anxiety for people since they not only want to look amazing and professional with what they wear, but still feel like themselves.

To minimize stress and maximize consistency, I have one piece of advice for you, shop your Branding Colors! If your colors are green, beige, and white, then when you walk into a store or shop online, search for items that are green, beige, and white, and stick to those colors.

> " To minimize stress and maximize consistency ... shop your Branding Colors! "

I often hear from our Community how liberating and simple shopping becomes now that they focus on buying certain colors. Branding Colors take the stress out of shopping and helps you feel more confident about your purchases and what you're wearing. When you wear your Branding Colors you get an extra boost of confidence. You get a little sparkle in your eye knowing that wearing your colors is an act of consistency and visually shows your Community what they can expect from you, which boosts their confidence in you.

Another benefit to a wardrobe full of your Branding Colors, is that it makes content creation a breeze. Whether it is a planned photoshoot, creating behind the scenes content, or snapping a spontaneous selfie, chances are, you are probably already wearing your Branding Colors! Then, when you share this content, there will be a visual consistency through the colors you are wearing.

Branding Colors are fun piece that illustrate your Connection-Based Brand. Be proud of your colors! Have fun and share them with your Community!

WARDROBE: STYLE

Another aspect of wardrobe is the type of clothes you decide to wear for a photoshoot. One of my photography clients loved wearing blazers and jeans. That was her go-to look. However, when it came time for her photoshoot, she asked, "Kels, I want to look professional, should I buy dresses and a formal suit?"

I looked at her and asked, "If you met up with a client today, would you wear a dress and a formal suit? Would that make sense?"

"Well, no, I never wear dresses, and I really only wear blazers with jeans."

I looked at her and said, "There is your answer. Wear blazers and jeans."

You don't need to change who you are and what you wear just because you're taking a photo. If you're a blazer and jeans person, but you wore a dress for photos, you wouldn't feel like you or look like you. You would come off as inauthentic by trying to be someone else. If you departed from your go-to style, it would also confuse your Community. They will feel less confident in you since you're departing from consistency, and now don't know what to expect from you.

Your wardrobe is a powerful tool to advance connection and confidence with your Community, so stay consistent with what makes sense to who you truly are. Stick to your style, stick to your colors, stick to you.

POSING

Posing for photos is an artform. It takes time and practice to really find your groove. To give you a kick start, I wanted to share a few important posing tips and posing no-no's I see both photographers and their subjects default to on the regular. It's my personal mission to help you unlearn these poses so you can come off as more real, approachable and ready to connect in your Lifestyle Branding photos.

POSE NO-NO 1: CROSSING ARMS

Unless you are a professional chef or in the fitness industry (an industry standard and acceptable pose), crossing your arms is a big no-no pose!

The crossing arms pose tells your audience you are closed off to business. You are closed off to opportunity. It tells your Community you are insecure and unwilling to open up to them and connect.

Unless you want to come off as unapproachable, open your arms in photos because it's a subconscious cue to your Community that you are here to serve, ready to connect and open for business and opportunity.

POSE NO-NO 2: HAND ON HIP

This is a pose everyone does. This is the safe pose. This is the standard pose to answer the "What do I do with my hands?" question or the safeguard against our arms looking gigantic. This pose maybe simple and convenient, but it also doesn't convey the confidence and leadership you want to share with your Community.

Whenever I see the hand on hip, I instantly think of a Las Vegas bachelorette party. It's not professional and doesn't allow you to illustrate your true personality. However, if crazy bachelorette party is your vibe and brand message, then go for it, but I challenge you to try something different.

Instead, try a pose with your hand in a pocket with your thumb out or place your hand on the side of your leg with your elbow back. You can even play with your hair, fix your collar, tweak your buttons, clap your hands, touch your hat, fiddle with your fingertips, or interact with items in your environment.

There can be a time and place for a hand on hip moment, but don't make it your go-to. You are a leader, so let your posing reflect your leadership.

THE GOLDEN RULE OF POSING

When properly posing for pictures (especially when you resist defaulting to the crossed arms or hand on hip poses) it can feel super awkward, and that is completely normal!

With photography, you are taking this 3D object (your body) and smashing it down into a 2D space (a photograph), so shaping and posing your body so you look approachable versus like you are taking a mugshot won't feel natural. It will feel completely awkward.

My golden rule of posing is, "If it feels awkward, you're doing it right." Awkward is normal. If you're feeling comfortable in a pose, it probably means your body is slouched or you have zero shape to your body. It's not a good look.

Get comfortable feeling awkward, and just know, the more you practice, the easier it will become! Now, go pop your hip, drop your shoulder, push your booty out, put your chin out and down, laugh it out, have fun and go slay your pose!

YOUR PHOTOGRAPHER

The fifth and final element of a successful Lifestyle Branding photoshoot is your photographer. Whether you are working with a professional or on a photo safari adventure with a friend taking pictures all over town on your phone, you need to team up with someone you can trust.

Being in front of a camera is a very vulnerable place to be, so partner with someone who understands this and will nurture and encourage you on your photoshoot.

Work with someone who:

⇨   Who notices details. Like when your hair is out of place, or your necklace is turned around.

⇨   Who won't be quiet behind the camera. Who will give direction and build up your confidence, not tear it down.

⇨   Who not only creates quality photos, but also delivers a quality experience.

⇨   Who has experience posing and directing bodies of all shapes and sizes.

⇨   Who can suggest the best locations, makeup, outfits, and props.

⇨   Who can tell your story with intentionality and life!

Working with your friends to create photos has its place, but it's absolutely worth it to invest in a professional Lifestyle Branding photographer who can make you feel confident in front of the camera, and who understands branding and how to visually tell your brand story with imagery. These photos will be your visual representation of your brand message, so it's important to work with someone who gets you and understands how to effectively illustrate that message.

ILLUSTRATE YOUR MESSAGE
Wrap Up

I know it is hard to get in front of the camera.

Whether you don't like being the center of attention, you struggle with body image, you want to lose that extra 10 or 20 pounds, you feel awkward or you feel lost, there are a million and one excuses for not showing up in photos. But in the end, excuses block you from connecting. These excuses block you from making your impact in your industry. You have to drop the excuses and visually show up for your Community.

The reality is, no matter what industry you are in, your Community buys into you first, not what you are selling. They want to see you. They want to connect to you. They want to connect to the humanity behind the brand. They want to connect to the heart. That's what creating and sharing custom imagery can do. It illustrates your Connection-Based Brand and provides a way to continue sharing the brand narrative you want to create.

From illustrating your Branding Words, to choosing the right colors, wearing a true-to-you wardrobe, to posing your body in a welcoming way, it all provides a way to share your story, connect with your Community and market your offering.

ILLUSTRATE YOUR MESSAGE

In this chapter you learned:

⇨ About Lifestyle Branding photoshoots

⇨ Photoshoot basics

⇨ How to define your Branding Colors

⇨ Photoshoot wardrobe tips

⇨ Posing tips

⇨ What to look for in a Lifestyle Branding Photographer

CHAPTER FOURTEEN

THE ONLY
MARKETING STRATEGY
YOU WILL EVER NEED

*"Good marketing offers us a view of the world. Bad
marketing offers a product to buy."*

- SIMON SINEK, AUTHOR

If traditional marketing's job is to deliver your message, Connection-Based Marketing is about delivering your message while simultaneously connecting with your Community and building/nurturing relationships. The way to successfully implement a Connection-Based Marketing strategy is integrating only one strategy, and that is to share value.

> " Connection-Based Marketing is about delivering your message while simultaneously connecting with your Community and building/nurturing relationships ... by sharing value. "

Sharing value is an evergreen marketing strategy that is applicable today, tomorrow and years from now. It is applicable to the current social media and marketing platforms of today and is applicable to the ones that haven't even been created yet. Providing value to your Community is the only marketing strategy you will ever need.

When you provide value, that's when you and your Community can shift focus from traditional, "Buy my stuff!!" marketing, to, "Let's connect first, build trust, foster a relationship, then, buy my stuff" mentality of Connection-Based Marketing. When you lead with value, you're opening the door to connect and impact.

THE 3 VALUE ELEMENTS OF BALANCED MARKETING

The biggest questions I get regarding marketing are, "What should I share?" and "What should I post?" and "What content should I create?"

The answer to all these questions is to create and share anything that provides value. Sharing value connects with, and enriches your Community.

Before sharing or creating anything, ask yourself this one key question, "How is this serving my Community?"

The answer ... provide value.

By providing value, it keeps your marketing and message simple and balanced. By leading with a value-first mentality, you can avoid falling into one of two common pitfalls most business owners and leaders land in when they start marketing. The two pitfalls are: *The Business Only Pitfall* and *The Over-Sharer Pitfall.*

The Business Only Pitfall. This is a person or business who solely delivers the message of business, business, business! This approach is devoid of human or personal elements. Their website, social media, print campaigns, etc., are only focused on what they sell and generally, full of random stock photos.

Realtors and individuals in Direct Sales (MLMs) are the guiltiest in this area. Most of the time their brokerage or parent company provides generic branded content they can just repost along with newly listed properties or new products.

If you look at their social media feed, their pages look like a carbon copy of everyone else in their industry. They are hiding behind the stock images and not stepping out and sharing what makes them different and unique (their Gap). All their marketing is generic, void of human connection.

The Over-Sharer Pitfall. This is the person shares too much of the personal. They open up their proverbial trench coat and expose too much of their personal life to the world. This way of marketing is self-focused, creates disconnect and feeds their ego vs serving others. Individuals that fall prey to this pitfall come across as inauthentic, insecure, and not interested in impacting and giving back to their overall Community. It's all about them, and not about providing value to others.

> " Before sharing or creating anything, ask yourself this one key question, how is this serving my Community? "

In order to have an effective marketing strategy and avoid the Business Only or Over Sharer pitfalls, you must focus on providing a balanced value-based marketing approach. Answer the one big question, "how is this serving my Community?" by sharing value and integrating the Three Value Elements of Balanced Marketing.

The Three Values Elements are:

1. Education Value

2. Emotional Value

3. Business Value

Whether you integrate these Three Value Elements into your social media, your website, your resume, project proposals, your podcast, blogs and beyond, by providing balanced value in your marketing and outreach, you will attract, serve, and retain individuals on your Attract List. You'll allow a genuine opportunity for your Community to connect with you, build trust and deeply buy into what you have to offer.

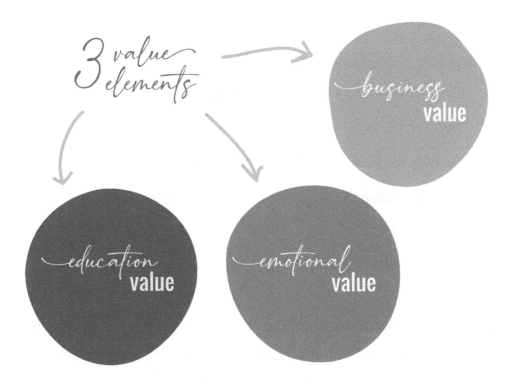

EDUCATION VALUE

This value element is exactly as it sounds, sharing elements of education with your Community.

You have spent time and energy learning about your specific skill, product or offering. You have become the expert and know more about this area than the Average Joe. This knowledge and experience are extremely valuable to your Community and provides a way to connect, deepen trust and establish your place as an expert in your industry.

Education Value is information that you can teach your Community, that enriches their lives and equips them to navigate their place in your industry.

Examples of Educational Value are:

⇨ Sharing answers to frequently asked questions

⇨ Tips and tricks

⇨ Creative hacks you have learned along the way

⇨ Sharing behind the scenes of in the moment learning opportunities

⇨ Tools to achieve their goals

You can share Educational Value on your social media, website, resume, or blogs. Educate your Community on social media or website. Educate a potential employer on your resume about areas of your expertise. You can create a print campaign or host events that reach and teach your Ideal Community. Education is the door opener to build trust, and establishes your place as the expert in your specific area of service.

EMOTIONAL VALUE

The second value element is Emotional Value. When I say emotional, I don't mean that you need to share stories that evoke tears or deep heartfelt words. You can, but Emotional Value is so much more than that. The Emotional Value is intended for you to share and touch on a broad spectrum of emotions, from heartfelt to funny to inspirational to real.

Examples of Emotional Value are:

⇨ Sharing personal stories

⇨ Sharing struggles and victories

⇨ Motivational quotes

⇨ Bloopers

⇨ Throwback stories + pictures

⇨ Inspirational moments + thoughts

⇨ Funny moments

⇨ Real moments

⇨ Behind the scenes moments

If your number one job is to connect with others, the Emotional Value element is where the deepest connection can happen. By stepping away from focusing solely on business and sharing the human side of your brand, your Community can see themselves in you.

By allowing a space to be personal while still being balanced with other value elements to your marketing, you can avoid being the Over Sharer pitfall. You can share personal elements, and not come off as self-focused or inauthentic because it is just a part (not the whole) of how you share and connect.

Just like Education Value, you can share Emotional Value on your social media, website, resume, or blogs. Share a personal story of how you got to where you are on your websites about me section or on your resume.

Share a funny story from your day on social media. Share something that inspires you on a blog or your podcast. Use the Emotional Value to weave the human element into your marketing to deepen genuine connection and trust.

BUSINESS VALUE

The final value of balanced marketing is sharing Business Value.

As a business owner or leader, you still must put your offering out there. You can't just educate, and you can't just share the emotional. You must remind people why you're showing up and what you're actually selling.

With integrating the other two Value Elements, Education and Emotional, into your marketing strategy, it helps you avoid the "Only Business" pitfall that so many fall into. Sharing what you offer/what you sell is vital to a business or career's success, but it can't be the main focus. There must be balance.

When you share all three Value Elements together you lay a foundation of connection through value that doesn't feel like you are oversharing or just being a sleazy salesperson, you're laying a foundation of broad value that people can connect with.

Examples of Business Value are:
- ⇨ Featured team members and/or clients
- ⇨ Sharing your offering
- ⇨ Calls to action
- ⇨ Business updates

⇨ Featured work

⇨ Client testimonials

⇨ New products/services/skills

⇨ Sales and deals

⇨ New hours

THE THIRD - THIRD - THIRD RULE

The Three Value Elements are here to help you create a Connection-Based Marketing plan that is balanced and leads with intentionality, not impulsivity. The best way to implement these Three Value Elements into your marketing strategy is to use the third-third-third rule.

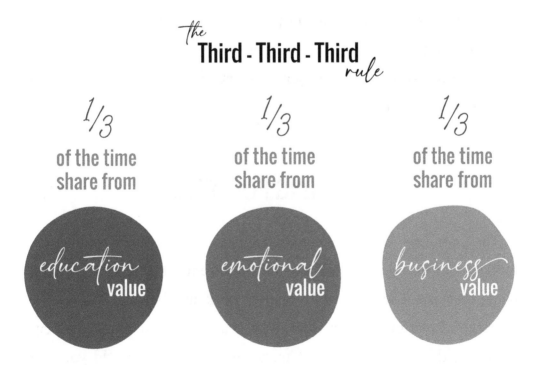

the
Third - Third - Third *rule*

1/3
of the time
share from

education **value**

1/3
of the time
share from

emotional **value**

1/3
of the time
share from

business **value**

That way, when you sit down to write a post, write website copy, or create any type of marketing content, you can look back at what you previously shared and determine what you should share next.

For example, for social media, look back at your last 3 posts and ask, "What value was I sharing in those posts?" If they were all business-business-business, then you know it's time to teach them something (Educational) or share a fun or moving moment (Emotional).

To keep things balanced, make sure each Value Element is getting equal amounts of visibility, and you're not heavy on just one.

Now of course, these Value Elements are not mutually exclusive, and you can blend them together. For example, you could start off a social media post with a funny story (Emotional Value) and then end with a call to action (Business Value). You could write a blog sharing new business hours (Business) and pair it with a picture of you and your puppy outside your store (Emotional).

Marketing with the Value Elements and using the third-third-third rule is a way to guide you, and keep your marketing intentional, balanced and primed for connection and building trust.

MARKETING PLATFORMS

The platforms where you can share these Three Value Elements and market your brand are seemingly infinite. From social media, websites, blogs, podcasts, courses, events, charity work, and beyond, you have no shortage of platforms from where you can share your brand message. However, the question is, what marketing platforms should you use? Which ones allow you to best connect and share your brand message?

The answer (as it is for any question you have) is to check back with your branding elements. Check back in with your Branding Words, Ideal Community, your Gap, and Niche, as well as the 5 Deciding Questions.

What platforms align with your Branding Words and will attract/build connection with your Ideal Community? What platforms would help advance your branding message with intentionality? Where do your 5 Deciding Questions tell you where to go?

Whether it is Instagram, Facebook, Twitter, or beyond, think about where your Community hangs out and what platform aligns with your Connection-Based Brand, and that's where you need to be.

MARKETING MIND GAMES

Putting yourself out there is scary. When you stop hiding behind your product, logo, branding visuals or the perfect business persona, and you step out as you, it's scary. When you take the brave step to share your Connection-Based Brand it opens the door to connect and make an impact in your Community, but also invites The Five Core Fears to show up with their friends, insecurity, and self-doubt.

The two biggest mind games that people can face when they put themselves out there are both rooted in Core Fear #1, the Fear of Others' Opinions. Specifically, 1) being afraid that they will be seen as a narcissist and/or 2) that they will get negative feedback from "haters" when they share and market their Connection-Based Brand.

Let's close out this chapter with addressing these two main Marketing Mind Games that can block you from stepping out and sharing your Connection-Based Brand.

MARKETING MIND GAME 1:
YOU ARE NOT A NARCISSIST

Because you have made it this far in *The Connection Method*, I know one thing for sure, you genuinely want to connect with and impact others. You want to lead with inspiration, not manipulation. You want to create impact in your Community because you truly care for others. You want to make a difference in the lives of others.

Are you nodding your head yes?

If you are, that means that you are not a narcissist.

It means you are not a self-indulgent person.

It means you have a bigger view of the world than just yourself.

Now why do I bring this up? Because this fear is the number one block or excuse, I hear from others for not wanting to put themselves out there with marketing on social media. They don't want to post pictures of themselves because they are afraid that people will think they are narcissistic and into themselves. They assume that people will just roll their eyes and say, "There she goes again! Another picture of herself! Who does she think she is?" Or "He really thinks he's the shit, doesn't he?"

Well, I am here to tell you that these fears are far from the actual truth.

The truth is, that when you post pictures of yourself, it's not conveying an "it's about me" message. No, when you post a picture of yourself with a caption full of value, it's conveying an "it's about you" message. When you do this, you're offering your hand out to connect. You are putting yourself out there and you are a vessel of connection.

Posting pictures of yourself is not about you—it's about them. It's about sharing an image that they can attach to, connect to, and feel seen in. Humans connect to humans, so you must show up in order to connect.

If you don't show up, that is a sure-fire way to have your Community forget about you and lose out on the opportunity to impact others. Don't be so closed off that people forget you are here. You have to step up, step out and show up in order to genuinely connect with your Community.

You are a vessel of connection.

Now I will say that you can tip into self-indulgence if you fall into the Over-Sharer pitfall that we just discussed. If you purely focus on posting from the Emotional Value, and share a message that's all about you with no value, and ignore the other two Value Elements, then yes, it will come off as very self-focused. If you do this, then what you have is *not* a Connection-Based Brand, what you have is a Self-Indulgent-Insecure Brand.

However, if you stick to sharing value and keep your marketing balanced with the Three Value Elements, and focus on serving your Community as a vessel of connection, then you don't need to worry one second about coming off as self-indulgent.

You will come off as caring, involved and a true leader.

Your Community is buying you first, and your offering second, so they need to be given the opportunity to connect with a real person, a real story, and real value, so it's time to ditch the narcissism fear and show up for your Community!

MARKETING MIND GAME 2:
HOW TO DEAL WITH HATERS

I am going to wrap up our marketing section with something that you will inevitably run into as you step out, build, and grow your Connection-Based Brand. Whether it is in-person haters or online trolls sending you negative comments and messages, you need to have a tangible game plan when negative energy enters your life.

A lot of people don't post on social media because they are afraid of what people will think, and afraid of getting inundated with online trolls telling them they are garbage. I wanted to quickly address this, so you are equipped with two things: 1) the truth and 2) an action plan for when, not if, you get hit with a hater nuclear strike (because that's how it feels when it happens).

THE TRUTH. Here's the truth, when you put yourself out there, it's not about you. It's about them. People see you as a vessel of connection that they use to connect with and see themselves.

Most people are looking for a positive light, so if you follow the above suggestions to keep your marketing message balanced with the Three Value Elements, then the majority of your feedback will be positive, empowering and uplifting.

The reality is that we are our biggest haters, and we tend to project our hater attitude onto others and assume everyone else feels the same way about you. Which is not the case. Focus on shifting your energy and attracting your Ideal Community by thinking and emulating the characteristics of your Attract List, and not the Repel List.

However, even though majority of the time people are searching for and want to give back support and positivity, there will inevitably come a time when you do get pricked with a negative comment, so then the Hater Action Plan kicks into action.

THE HATER ACTION PLAN

Unfortunately, we don't live in rainbow and sunshine land where unicorns serve you sparkling lemonade and tell you how incredible you are. Nope, we live in the real world, so there will come a time when you receive negative and hurtful messages, comments, or gossip about you. I guarantee it. It will happen.

When it does happen, do you have a plan of attack?

I find that if I have a process to tackle negativity before it happens, I don't simmer in it, and am able to turn that negativity into motivating power. Just like defining our brand, we must take the emotional and turn it into something tangible and define a real process to deal with real emotions and circumstances. The world needs your voice, so we can't let negativity get us down for long.

Here is your four step Hater Action Plan when negative people or comments come into your world.

STEP 1: FEEL THE FEELS

Yeah, it hurts. The comment, the message, the snide remark. It hurts. Allow it to hurt. Feel the feels. Don't disregard them. They are there for

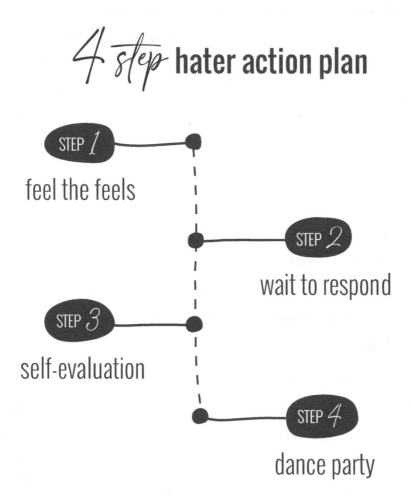

4 step hater action plan

STEP 1
feel the feels

STEP 2
wait to respond

STEP 3
self-evaluation

STEP 4
dance party

a reason, so feel them. To help you process the feels, you should allow yourself to vent to a trusted friend or mentor. Get the feelings out of your head by talking about them and acknowledging them.

STEP 2: WAIT TO RESPOND

When we are in the thick of hurt, it is so easy to lash out right away. But this is not how we stay classy and rise above the circumstance. Do not respond right away. Let the feelings, anger, and hurt mellow. Sleep on it. Wait. Gather yourself. A hot mess, emotional filled clapback is not a good look for anyone. Feel the feels. Breathe. Talk to a trusted friend or mentor. Wait.

STEP 3: SELF EVALUATION

Before responding (if you even choose to respond at all), it's time to do a self-evaluation. Even if the comment hurts, there may actually be a thread of truth sewn in. There may be an opportunity you can grow from.

Complete a self-evaluation, and ask yourself:

"What type of energy have I been putting out?"

"Did my energy—or the way I've been presenting myself—open the door to this type of negativity?"

"Is there anything truth in what they said?"

Once you have done this, then ask yourself, "Is this person projecting their hurt onto me?"

First, evaluate and take responsibility for your own energy and then check in with empathy. You never know what's going behind closed doors for others, so allow yourself to shift the perspective from your hurt to their circumstance. Hurt is a strong emotion, but empathy and kindness are superhero level emotions that have the power to take you to new levels of understanding and maturity. Sometimes this negativity is tied to a much bigger story of pain and insecurity, and sometimes, people are just assholes who love to bring others down. Decide which one they are and if there is a place for your own personal growth.

STEP 4: DANCE PARTY

Once you have completed steps 1-3 of the Hater Action Plan, now it's time for my favorite part ... the dance party! Yes, I said dance party!

It's time to *celebrate* this hater message because it means that your message and your mission is reaching beyond just your immediate circle. Your message is going out beyond your comfort zone, making an impact, and connecting with others on a broader level.

When you start receiving hater messages it confirms that you are doing something right, so keep going. Don't let one person ruin it for the rest of your Community. Your voice has value and needs to be heard. Keep going.

MARKETING STRAETGY
Wrap Up

Connection-Based Marketing is intended for you to deliver your branding message while simultaneously attracting, connecting, and building relationships with your Community. Leverage Connection-Based Marketing by sharing value. Stay balanced in your marketing by implementing the Three Value Elements and the third-third-third rule. Connect with your Community not just solely on the business side or just the over-sharing personal side, but knit together a marketing strategy that integrates education, emotional and business value elements equally.

Choose marketing platforms that align with your branding elements. Check back in with your Branding Words and where your Community will be best served. There are a lot of options and paths to take for your marketing, so don't get distracted by the shiny, stay consistent with your Connection-Based Brand.

Don't get distracted by the fear of putting yourself out there. Remember to focus on your Community, not your competition. Don't focus on what everyone else is doing, focus on your voice and serving your Community with what you uniquely offer. Sharing you is selfless, not selfish.

" Sharing you is selfless, not selfish. "

Your Community has been waiting for you to step out, own your space, and share it with them. Yes, there will be haters out there ready to slap duct tape over your mouth or who get joy out of making you feel small, but don't let them win. Use your Hater's Action Plan and push on. Remember that you always have more supporters than haters. Don't let the few negative voices diminish the positive. Don't let them silence your voice. Your voice has value, your Community needs to hear it. Now go step out, be a vessel of connection, and deliver your message!

MARKETING STRATEGY

In this chapter you learned:

⇨   That the secret to creating a timeless and effective marketing strategy is to provide value to your Community.

⇨   About having balanced marketing strategy by implementing The Three Value Elements.

⇨   The Three Value Elements of a balanced marketing strategy are
- Education
- Emotional
- Business

⇨   About sharing the Three Value Elements using the third-third-third rule.

⇨   That if you put yourself and your Connection-Based Brand out there, you are not self-indulgent, but actually a vessel of connection for others to feel seen.

⇨   About the Haters Action Plan and what to do when you experience negative comments, messages, or gossip.

CHAPTER FIFTEEN

ACTION PLAN

Your good enough—is good enough.

It's December 2020, and I am sitting in a hotel suite at a lodge in the mountains of Washington state. There is a gentle dusting of snow on the evergreen trees outside my window, the lodge is quiet, my cozy fireplace is flickering, and my Wonder Woman mug is close by, full of hot tea. It's the most perfect setting.

I've come to this picturesque place for a writing retreat to finish the book you are now holding. After nearly 3 years of hard work, I finally see the finish line.

It has been a long process to get here. Developing and testing out *The Connection Method* process with countless, real life entrepreneurs and leaders took years and a lot of trial and error. However, the biggest thing that delayed my progress was my inner voice telling me that this book needed to be perfect. Perfectionism blocked me from pushing forward and paralyzed me from writing and kept me second guessing everything and overthinking like a twitchy squirrel.

However, I am so appreciative I had my author/book coach Jocelyn to hold my hand through the process. She always said, "Kelsey, if you strive for perfect, it will never get done, it just needs to be good enough! Because your good enough—is good enough." I took this to heart and made it my mantra to help me finish this book.

While on my retreat, "Good enough is good enough" kept circling in my brain, and then in a magical turn of events, was beautifully illustrated to me, in real life, on my first night at the lodge. But first, let me take you back a few decades ...

When I was 13 years old, I took my first figure skating lesson. I was hooked, and quickly dove into the world of competitive figure skating. Skating was the first sport where I felt seen. I felt like I could be myself without fear of being bullied. Skating made me feel like I belonged, and I wasn't an outcast anymore. I had a place. I mattered. I learned technical skills, but also had the freedom to be creative and artistic on the ice.

Now in my 30s, figure skating has remained my emotional and physical outlet. It still allows me to connect with myself and express myself in the rawest form. It's the place I feel most myself and at peace.

So, when I learned that the lodge where I was staying for my writing retreat had an outdoor skating rink, I was beyond excited! Skating on an outdoor rink had been on my bucket list for nearly 20 years!

The lodge staff graciously arranged for me to have private ice time that evening, and as I walked up to the rink that night, it was nothing short of magical. Snow lightly fell from the stary night sky and the rink was illuminated with warm twinkle lights stretched across like an incandescent ceiling.

As I laced up my skates, the ice rink team told me the ice conditions were rough and spongy, and not ideal for technical skating. As I stepped on the ice, and feeling the ice on my blades, I saw that they were right, the ice was not ideal. For safety, I decided against performing any big spins or jumps. I needed to keep my skate basic.

My Crew on Instagram were eagerly waiting with anticipation to see how my skate went. Even though I was disappointed that I wasn't able to share video of me performing technical skills, I set my tripod up and recorded my basic skate anyway.

Despite my less-than-ideal performance, it was still an unforgettable experience, so went ahead and shared clips of my skate to Instagram. I paired it with a beautiful song from Andrea Bocelli and didn't expect much of a reaction since it was just me skating around sticking to basic moves. However, the messages I received after posting shocked me.

"This was so beautiful to watch."

"This was so inspiring! Thank you for sharing this magical moment with us!"

"I am so inspired now!"

"I love seeing you shine!"

"You are brilliant! I didn't know you could do that!"

"This makes me cry, it's so beautiful!"

I was shocked by these messages. Since I couldn't do any impressive, showstopping moves, I didn't think anyone would care or be impacted. However, my Crew proved me wrong. Even though it was basic and far from perfect, it impacted and inspired them and touched their hearts. It connected.

What I did was simple, imperfect, and a little clumsy, but it was good enough.

It wasn't perfect, but it was still impactful.

My good enough was good enough.

WHERE DO WE GO FROM HERE?

My good enough was good enough, and your good enough is good enough.

This is the mindset I want you to remember as you head out into the world with your newly defined Connection-Based Brand.

Your good enough is good enough.

It doesn't have to be perfect.

You don't have to be perfect (in fact, please don't).

It doesn't have to be a showstopper or Olympic level to deeply connect with others. You just have to show up as you are and share your Connection-Based Brand with others.

Throw the idea of perfection out the window in order to successfully share, grow and build your brand. As you move forward out into the real world with your Connection-Based Brand, your action plan is simple—

own who you are and don't apologize for it. Share your Connection-Based Brand with pride!

> " Your action plan is simple—
> own who you are and don't apologize for it. "

ACTION PLAN

BRANDING WORDS

Let your Branding Words be your compass, map, guide, and filter for *everything*. Take ownership of them and make them your own. Live them out. Speak them. Keep them in front of you. Print them up and frame them. Make them your desktop or phone wallpaper background. Write your Words on sticky notes and put them everywhere.

Use your Branding Words to make decisions. Use them to decide what to wear and how to present yourself. Use them to share with your Community about who you are, what you value and what people can expect from you. Use them to tell your Community how they should perceive you and speak about you.

Let your Branding Words be your leader. Filter everything through them. They are your foundation and the way to stay consistent.

IDEAL COMMUNITY

Your impact is more powerful when you keep your focus on your Attract List. Don't spend precious time appeasing everyone and serving your Repel List. Use your Attract List to attract a Community who energize you and support you. Repel people who don't.

Your Ideal Community is waiting for you to focus your time and attention on serving them, so don't get distracted or swayed by the Repel List-ers. Use your Attract List to make sure your own energy is consistent with who you want to attract, so you don't end up on you own Repel List.

THE GAP

The Gap is what makes you different. Your Gap in the line has been waiting for you. It has your name on it. Don't let a seemingly saturated industry deter you from your purpose.

This is the time to step into your Gap and own your place. This is the time to cinch down your backpack full of the powerful things that make you unique (your Sasquatch Factor) and confidently own your place in line.

Your Gap is the biggest source of connection for others to feel seen by you and your story, so share it. It's not selfish to share your story, it's selfless.

NICHE

Define what area you specialize in. Define where you are the expert.

Don't try to do it all. Don't say yes to everything. Define your area of expertise and stay there.

Focus on one or two areas and create depth and a solid footing there versus spreading yourself too thin. When you spread yourself too thin, it creates something unstable and fragile, so invest your time and energy into building depth, stability and expertise in your specific Niche.

There is more than enough to go around. Say no to opportunities that don't align with your Niche so others in your industry can benefit from them. Focus on your Niche, and invest yourself in that space.

VALUE PROPOSITION

Don't reinvent the wheel every time someone asks, "What do you do?" Stay consistent with your message and expressing how you serve. Use your Branding Words, Ideal Community, Niche and end result to guide you. Speak and share with intentionality.

THE 5 DECIDING QUESTIONS

Use these questions to help manage overthinking and give you action steps for what opportunities to take, choices to make and help you give you clear and intentional direction.

Keep these questions on hand and at the ready to make decisions. These help you stay consistent and validate the decisions you make. Filter opportunities through these questions in order to make confident and consistent decisions that propel you forward and not hold you back.

1. Does this opportunity, circumstance or thought coordinate, encourage, promote and/or align with my Branding Words?

2. Does this opportunity, circumstance or thought attract my Ideal Community? Will it attract the kind of people that will energize, excite and uplift me?

3. Does this opportunity cater to, serve, or provide value to those in your Ideal Community searching for solutions in my specific Niche/what I specialize in?

4. If I say yes to this opportunity, circumstance or thought, will I feel good about promoting it and sharing that I was involved with it?

5. If I DON'T say yes to this opportunity, circumstance or thought, how will I feel? If I DO say yes, how will I feel?

CONNECTION-BASED MARKETING

The number one rule for Connection-Based Marketing is to provide value. Before creating any marketing ask yourself, "how is this serving my Community?" Let this question along with providing value guide your marketing decisions.

Create content that is personal and custom to you by illustrating your message with Lifestyle Branding photography.

Define your own Branding Colors and integrate them into everything, your marketing materials, social media, website, wardrobe and beyond.

Share your message while simultaneously connecting and building relationships with your Community. That's the key to connection.

ALWAYS COME BACK TO
The Connection Method

This book is meant to be a reusable tool for growth. Your life, business and career will flex and change overtime, so when you are experiencing times of transition, overwhelm, or confusion, come back to this book. Come back to the questions to help you get back in touch with who you are. Come back to the actionable steps to give you clarity. Come back to *The Connection Method* to help you find your new direction and remind you of why you are here. Come back so you can reconnect.

NOW IS THE TIME

With your Connection-Based Brand, you now have all the tools you need to grow your brand an become a Connection-Based Leader. You're equipped to make an impact, bring humanity back to business and leave a lasting legacy. Your Community is waiting to connect with you, your brand message, and your story, you just have to get out of your own way. Stop asking and start acting.

> " Stop asking and start acting. "

To ignite the process of connection, you must take action and launch your Connection-Based Brand. Starting is the hardest part because the Fear of the Unknown runs wild at the starting line. Once you do take off, you will quickly learn that sharing your Connection-Based Brand is what your Community has been waiting for. Even if it feels new, awkward, and imperfect, the brand you've created is more than good enough.

Fear will always be there, but now you know how to define and name the fears that are clawing at your back. Call them out by name and send them to the back seat. You won't let fear control you or paralyze you anymore. You have the tools to move forward.

You now have a clear path to achieve your end goal. An end goal that creates a brand culture and legacy that can inspire and live beyond you. By connecting with yourself first in order to connect with others, you have created a Connection-Based Brand that equips you to stay consistent, feel confident, give you direction and most of all, connect with others.

Your Connection-Based Brand will lead you to the thing you came here to do, and that is to *connect* so others can *feel seen, feel heard, and know they matter*. You're equipped and ready!

Now go, we're waiting for you!

JOIN THE
CONNECTION CREW

Use the hashtag **#TheConnectionMethod** to share your experience going through the book with your Connection Crew community!

If you would like to share your story to us directly, send us an email at **mystory@kelseykurtis.com**

To share the message of connection with your Community, check out The Connection Crew Collection at

www.kelseykurtis.com/shop

Follow Kelsey on social media

@kelseymkurtis

AKNOWLEGEMENTS

My first and forever thanks go to Jocelyn Lindsay, my author/book coach, the person who inspired *The Connection Method* and helped carry me to publication (and beyond).

I first met Jocelyn at one of my speaking engagements, where afterwards she asked me to help her create a brand for her new business as an author coach. Little did we know that the branding process I would create to help her would turn into *The Connection Method*, and full circle, use her incredible leadership and talent as an author coach to help me complete this book. It was serendipitous we came together, and I am forever grateful for her friendship, guidance, encouragement and laugh-till-we-cry time together. Thank you JL, you're the reason this book exists.

Secondly, I want to send bucket loads of thanks to the original beta testers of *The Connection Method*. They signed on before I had an organized system. They signed on before I knew what I was doing or even had a name for what I was creating. They were the ones who allowed me to ask the deep questions and trusted me with their honest answers. It took 3 years, but we did it. Thank you, Rachelle, Megan, Jocelyn, Serina, Candace, Brandi, Kyla, Chelsea, and Jasmin and Aldo.

Finally, I would like to thank you, my incredible Connection Crew. Thank you for sharing the message of *The Connection Method* and Connection-Based Branding!

You're the ones doing the work to step out from behind perfection in order to bring humanity back to business with your leadership. You're the ones who are inspiring and creating a positive impact in your Community. You're the ones stepping out of your comfort zone and sharing your voice, story, and Connection-Based Brand message so others can feel seen, feel heard and know that they matter. You're the ones who didn't let fear stop you from going out and sharing your message and following your purpose.

You're the rock stars. You deserve all the thanks and cozy Branding Mama hugs. Thank you for your support, courage, and ambition. Thank you to my treasured Connection Crew!

Thank you.

GLOSSARY *of Terms*

GLOSSARY OF TERMS

Badass: Someone who pushes past fear in order to pursue their calling and purpose. Synonyms: you.

The Sasquatch Factor: The things about us that makes us feel different, like an outsider or even a curiosity. These things can be completely obvious, something outwardly physical, or something more deeply rooted within our hearts. It's what makes us unique and makes up the foundation of who we are.

Connection: Creating a relational tie between a human and another thing such as a person, place, business, product, message, item, or story. The truest form of connection comes from when others can see themselves in you.

Consistency: An action repeated in the same way. The spark for confidence to build.

Cocky: A behavior and mindset rooted out of insecurity.

Confident: A behavior and mindset rooted out of authenticity and consistency.

Intention: Doing something on purpose, or deliberate.

Impact: Having a palpable effect on someone or something in order to inspire a shift in perspective or cause tangible change.

Brand: Composed of three essential elements: your brand foundation, brand visuals, brand logo. Your brand is your message.

Brand Foundation: A Brand Foundation is the perceived emotional image of a business or individual, which encompasses, who they are, what they value, what others can expect, and their overall mission.

Brand Visuals: The visual elements to represent your brand.

Brand Logo: A simple design marker representing your brand in icon form.

Brand Elements: The elements that you've defined for your Connection-Based Brand.

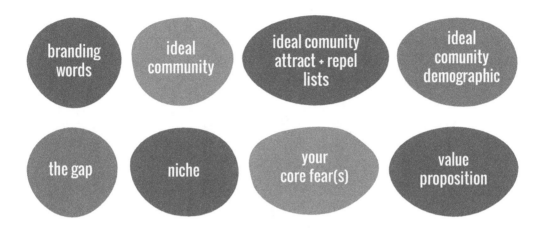

Branding Battle Bag: A powerful weapon against overthinking and self-doubt. It is your tool kit to direct you, to get you out of your own way, to validate you, and help you to make confident decisions so you can move forward and progress in life and business! Currently in your Branding Battle Bag are your defined branding elements; your Branding Words, your Ideal Community Attract + Repel Lists, your Gap, your Niche, your Value Proposition, and your Core Fear(s).

Connection-Based Brand: A Connection-Based Brand is about bringing humanity back to business and allowing the personal to form the foundation of your brand message. Connection-Based Branding is founded on one simple concept, that the truest form of connection comes from when others can see themselves in you. So, in order to genuinely connect and create impact, you first have to get in touch with you.

Connection-Based Brand Evolution: Maps out the future potential growth and impact trajectory of your Connection-Based Brand.

Connection-Based Leader: A vessel of connection, as a source to inspire others to grow and achieve more. As a Connection-Based Leader, you have the opportunity to be a beacon of light for someone, when they might not receive it from anywhere else.

The Connection Crew: A group of individuals who define and share a Connection-Based Brand for their business or leadership role. They are committed to bring humanity back to business by bringing in the personal side to their professional world. They are committed to do this in order for others can feel seen, feel heard and know that they matter, and in turn creating impact in their Community.

Core Value Examples

Accountability	Justice
Collaboration	Kindness
Commitment	Leadership
Community	Loyalty
Consistency	Open-Mindedness
Curiosity	Optimism
Dependability	Passion
Discipline	Patience
Diversity	Peace
Education	Perseverance
Efficiency	Positivity
Excellence	Quality
Faith	Reliability
Family	Responsibility
Freedom	Service
Honesty	Teamwork
Hope	Transparency
Innovation	Trust
Integrity	Truth

Branding Words: 3-5 words or phrases that define who you are, what you value and what others can expect from you. They are the foundation for your brand, brand message and is the filter for *everything* you do.

Branding Word Sub-Words: Words that support a main Branding Word.

Branding Word Set: Is a Branding Word that is a combination of two words. A Word Set is when you combine two words in order to specifically define the type of word you are describing. Only allow ONE in your Branding Word list.

Core Branding Word: This is the word in your Branding Word list that represents the essence of who you are and what you value and what people can expect. The word that is steadfast and represents the core of everything you stand for.

Branding Word Examples

Accessible	Calm
Adventurous	Care
Advisor*	Casual
Ambitious	Clarity
Approachable	Classic
Body-Positive	Classy
Bold	Clean

Clever	Dramatic
Comfortable	Edgy
Commitment	Education*
Communication*	Elegant
Community*	Empathy
Compassion	Empower*
Confidence	Energetic
Connection*	Energy
Conservative	Excellence*
Contemporary	Exclusive
Consistency/Consistent	Experienced*
Courage	Feminine
Craft	Fresh
Creative	Friendly
Custom	Fun
Culture	Funky
Dedicated	Fun-Loving
Dependable	Genuine
Diligent	Glamorous
Direct	Goal-Driven

Grounded

Health/Healthy

Helpful

Honest

Humorous

Imaginative

Innovative*

Insight

Inspiration/Inspire*

Instinctual

Integrity*

Intuitive

Joy/Joyful

Leader*

Leadership

Loyal

Luxurious/Luxury

Magnetic

Masculine

Maverick

Mysterious

Non-Judgmental

Original

Passion

Peace

Polished*

Positive

Powerhouse

Precise

Proactive

Quirky

Radiance

Real*

Rebellious/Rebel

Refined

Relatable

Relationships

Relaxed

Resilient

Resource*

Retro

Rugged

Safe-Haven

Simple

Solutions*

Southern

Spicy

Spiritual

Steady

Tenacious

Timeless

Tough

Traditional

Transparency

Trust*

Trustworthy

Unique

Vigilante

Warm

Welcoming

Witty

Ideal Community: Represents the positive, respectful, and supportive people you want to attract to your circle. It is composed of three groups, your Ideal Client, your Ideal Team, Ideal Leadership, and Ideal support Crew.

Ideal Client: Is an individual, group of people or employer who your work is directly serving.

Ideal Team: Composed of individuals or teams of people who help you run your business and/or help you do your job. They can be employees, contractors, colleagues, team members or support staff.

Ideal Leadership: An individual or resource who pours into your growth as a leader. The Ideal Leadership role can be composed of mentors, corporate leadership, educators, spiritual leaders, authors, public figures, speakers, etc. Ideal Leadership can appear in the form of one-on-one interactions or even resources such as a podcasts, books, blogs, social medias, videos, conferences, or online courses.

Ideal Support Crew: Composed of your closest family and friends. They are the ones you go to for rest, venting and celebration. They are your sounding board and the ones who keep you grounded as your success and impact grows. They are essential and non-negotiable. They are your Ideal Support Crew.

Attract List: A list of the 5-10 characteristics of individuals who you want to *attract* to your Ideal Community and serve with your offering.

Attract Listers: The people who represent and reflect the characteristics of your Attract List.

Repel List: A list of the 5-10 characteristics of individuals who you want to *repel* from your Ideal Community and serve with your offering.

Repel Listers: The people who represent and reflect the characteristics of your Repel List.

The Gap: What makes you different. Your personal history, personal qualities and professional qualities that make you, your story, and your brand unique.

Niche: The specific area in your industry where you serve, what you specialize in, and what you are the expert in

Value Proposition: Your Value Proposition is how you simply communicate your Connection-Based Brand message when you are asked "what do you do?"

Value Proposition Equation: Branding Words + Ideal Community + Niche + Value Gained or End Result = VALUE PROPOSITION

The Five Core Fears

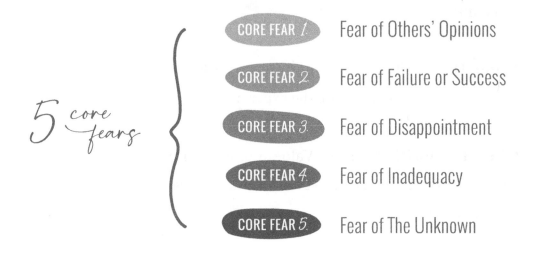

5 core fears {

CORE FEAR 1.   Fear of Others' Opinions

CORE FEAR 2.   Fear of Failure or Success

CORE FEAR 3.   Fear of Disappointment

CORE FEAR 4.   Fear of Inadequacy

CORE FEAR 5.   Fear of The Unknown

The Five Deciding Questions: Are the 5 questions you must ask yourself before making any decision to help you stay consistent and intentional.

Does this opportunity, circumstance or thought coordinate, encourage, promote and/or align with my Branding Words?

Does this opportunity, circumstance or thought attract my Ideal Community? Will it attract the kind of people that will energize, excite, and uplift me?

Does this opportunity cater to, serve, or provide value to those in my Ideal Community who are searching for solutions in my specific Niche?

If I say yes to this opportunity, circumstance or thought, will I feel good about promoting it and sharing that I was involved with it?

If I DON'T say yes to this opportunity, circumstance or thought, how will I feel? If I DO say yes, how will I feel?

Connection-Based Marketing: Delivering your message while simultaneously connecting with your Community and building/nurturing relationships by sharing value.

Connection-Based Marketing Cycle: A way to keep your branding message, visuals, and marketing consistent.

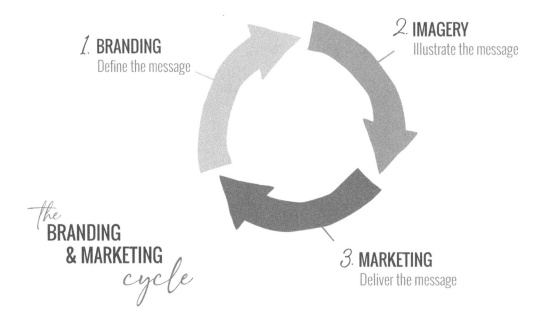

1. BRANDING
Define the message

2. IMAGERY
Illustrate the message

3. MARKETING
Deliver the message

the BRANDING & MARKETING *cycle*

Personal Branding Photography: Illustrates the person(s) behind the brand. It is a creative take on headshots. Most of the time these photos are done in a studio and are straight forward images of the person behind the business.

Lifestyle Branding Photography: Includes elements of Personal Branding photography, but also illustrates the lifestyle of the person/people behind the business. Lifestyle Branding captures images of what it looks like to work with an individual. It shares the personality and illustrates who they are apart from the professional world. The purpose of Lifestyle Branding is to create even more in-depth connection pieces between you and your Community via intentional story-focused imagery.

No-No Poses: Crossed arms and hand on hip. Try to stay away from defaulting to these poses in order to show confident leadership, unless the poses make sense for the specific brand.

The Golden Rule of Posing: If you feel awkward, you're doing it right.

The Three Value Elements of Balanced Marketing: Educational Value, Emotional Value and Business Value. These values are not mutually exclusive and can be combined when creating content.

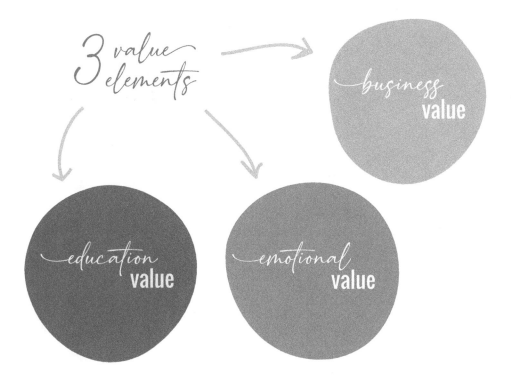

The Third-Third-Third Rule for Balanced Marketing: Helps you share the Three Value Elements of Balanced Marketing that is not too self-focused or business-focused. In order for balanced marketing, a third of the time, share Education Value, a third of the time share Emotional Value, and a third of the time, post Business Value.

Hater Action Plan: A predetermined plan to help you respond to negative comments and messages to help keep your mindset from overthinking and ignoring the positivity in your Community.

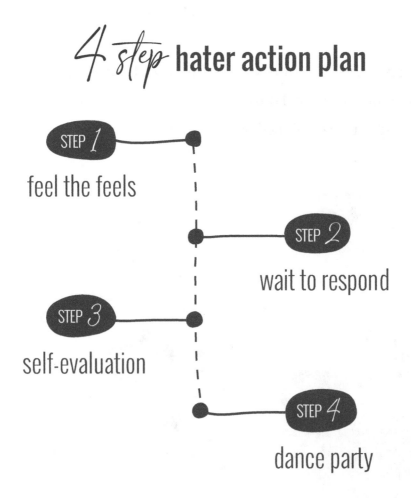

4 step hater action plan

STEP 1
feel the feels

STEP 2
wait to respond

STEP 3
self-evaluation

STEP 4
dance party

Branding Color Meanings

BEIGE: Neutral, Calm, Relaxing, Dependable, Comfort.

BLACK: Formal, Dramatic,Excellence, Sophistication, Security, Power, Elegance, High End.

BLUE: Trust, Peace, Loyalty, Competence, Wisdom, Intelligence, Depth, Stability.

BROWN: Rugged, Dependable, Trustworthy, Simple, Grounded.

BURGUNDY: Sophistication, Luxury, High End, Power, Ambition. A shade of red.

CORAL: Warmth, Acceptance, Outgoing, Dynamic. A perfect combination of pink and orange.

GOLD: Opulence, Luxury, Extravagance, Wealth, Status, Abundance.

GREEN: Nature, Freshness, Growth, Harmony, Health, Healing, Quality.

GREY: Neutrality, Indifference, Conservative, Reserve, Grounded, Foundational, Solid.

GOLD: Opulence, Luxury, Extravagance, Wealth, Status, Abundance.

GREEN: Nature, Freshness, Growth, Harmony, Health, Healing, Quality.

GREY: Neutrality, Indifference, Conservative, Reserve, Grounded, Foundational, Solid.

HOT PINK: Rebel, Assertive, Energy, Attention. A shade of pink.

MAROON: Confidence, Ambition, Creativity, Risk, Excitement. A shade of purple.

MAUVE: Devotion, Renewal, Youth, Purity, Idealistic, Romantic. A shade of purple.

MINT: Refreshing, Inviting, Tranquil, Innocence. A shade of green.

NAVY: Power, Authority, Serious, Truth, Stable, Traditional. A shade of blue.

ORANGE: Enthusiasm, Success, Creativity, Adventure, Confidence, Bravery, Social, Warmth, Fun.

PINK: Compassion, Sincerity, Friendship, Sweet, Approachable, Sophistication, Playful.

PURPLE: Balance, Spirituality, Dignity, Wisdom, Independence, Ambition, Opulence, Luxury, Royal.

RED: Excitement, Love, Energy, Strength, Passion, Danger, Power, Sexy, Spicy.

SILVER: Sleek, Modern, Glamorous, Elegant, Sophisticated, High Tech.

TEAL: Commitment, Trust, Balance, Protection, Rational, Practical. A perfect blend of blue and green—an elevated version of Turquoise.

TURQUOISE: Calm, Growth, Energy, Uplifting. A perfect blend of blue and green.

WHITE: Clean, Simple, Honest, Sincere, Brilliance, Illumination.

YELLOW: Creativity, Happiness, Positivity, Warmth, Cheer, Joy, Positive, Enthusiasm.

ABOUT THE AUTHOR

Kelsey Kurtis is a branding educator, professional lifestyle branding photographer, author, energetic speaker, and unapologetic cheerleader for leaders in business. She is the author of *The Connection Method®* and creator of Connection-Based Branding.

Kelsey has over ten years of experience as a professional photographer and working with business owners and leaders. She is passionate about educating and equipping leaders with the tools they need to genuinely connect with both themselves and their audience empowering them to impact their community.

Kelsey is based out of the Pacific Northwest in Bellingham, Washington and enjoys traveling, standup comedy, figure skating, watching classic '90s movies, eating tacos and gummy bears, and most of all, spending time laughing with her close friends.

The best way to connect with Kelsey is on social media where she shares encouraging, educational and entertaining content. Follow Kelsey across all platforms at:

@kelseymkurtis

To learn more about Kelsey, working with her, speaking engagements, media inquiries, or accessing the most up-to-date resources, please visit her website at:

www.KelseyKurtis.com